THE
HEARTBEAT
COOKBOOK

THE HEARTBEAT COOKBOOK

TOM BRIDGE

With original illustrations by Gerry Halpin

CASSELL

ACKNOWLEDGEMENTS

The author would like to thank everyone at Yorkshire Tyne Tees, especially Jacqui Williams. Thanks are also due to my favourite artist Gerry Halpin for his help and advice throughout the book, and to Keith and Jean Richardson and everyone at the Goathland Hotel, who make the world's best crab sandwiches and roast beef with Yorkshire pudding. Finally, special thanks to Phil Walsh , Tom and Kate Jackson and all the wonderful people of Yorkshire who helped inspire my recipes.

First paperback edition 1995 by
Cassell
Wellington House
125 Strand
London WC2R 0BB

Distributed in the United States
by Sterling Co., Inc.
387 Park Avenue South
New York, NY 10016-8810

Distributed in Australia
by Capricorn Link (Australia) Pty Ltd
2/13 Carrington Road
Castle Hill
NSW 2154

British Library Cataloguing-in-Publication Data
A catalogue record of this book is available from the British Library

ISBN 0-304-34704-3

Designed and typset by Blackjacks

Printed and bound in Great Britain by Bath Colour Books Ltd

Photographic credits: All photographs © Yorkshire Tyne Tees Television except front cover background, pp16-17, pp40-41, pp104-105, pp128-129 David Ward

Contents

Foreword
by Nick Berry

To millions of viewers, Heartbeat country – the North Riding of Yorkshire thirty years ago – has become a reality. But you don't need to travel back in time to appreciate the glories of Yorkshire. The largest county in England, it has every type of English scenery in abundance – moorlands and uplands, rich plains and vales, and the spectacular North sea coastline – all just as beautiful today as in 1965!

Rich countryside produces rich food – and the food traditions of Yorkshire are second to none: hams, pies, lamb, game, salmon, trout, seafood, not to speak of pure waters to brew the finest Yorkshire beers. Add to these the famous Yorkshire home cooking – scones, breads and the world renowned Yorkshire pudding – and you'll see just how important we thought it was that you should be able to taste the flavours of Heartbeat country as well as enjoying the stories, characters and atmosphere of the Heartbeat series.

In this book, Tom Bridge, master chef and food historian, has brought together 150 mouthwatering Heartbeat country recipes to take you through the seasons. And who better? If only because – despite being born on the wrong side of the Pennines to play cricket for Yorkshire – Tom spent much of his own childhood in 1960s Yorkshire and has special memories of the home cooking of that time. From spring lamb to autumn game birds, winter warmers for raw November days, and a full Aidensfield Christmas dinner, The *Heartbeat Country Cookbook* really has got something for everyone.

Enjoy your food!

Nick Berry

Introduction

Having spent most of working life in kitchens around Britain, I really never considered the power behind the food around Yorkshire. During my visits to the home of my friend, Phil Walsh, who lives in the picturesque town of Shipley, we toured Yorkshire together, enjoying the food and drink in restaurants, pubs and inns around this beautiful part of the English countryside. We also enjoyed the outstanding scenic views and the warm welcome from the people of Yorkshire.

Being a very keen *Heartbeat* viewer, I had to visit Goathland near Whitby to get the right feel for the *Heartbeat Country Cookbook*. The landscape around this area is more varied than any other region of the British Isles. The views are breathtaking. To see a steam train racing through the valley, sheep grazing on the moors without a worry in the world, the peace and tranquillity is so absolute it came as quite a shock to see several hundred *Heartbeat* fans clamouring around the Goathland Hotel (which in *Heartbeat* is the Aidensfield Arms,) to get a glimpse of my favourite character Claude Greengrass(played by Bill Maynard) with his dog Alfred.

The *Heartbeat Cookbook* contains a selection of mouthwatering recipes from the homes and hearths of Yorkshire. There are twelve chapters of delicious recipes, ranging from Springtime in the heart of the moors, through to summer picnics, barbecues and traditional Christmas fare. The wide selection of lunch recipes made the *Heartbeat* cast gasp with delight at the sumptious choice of food Yorkshire can produce, from Whitby Potted Shrimps, Toad inth' 'Ole, Yorkshire Bacon Cakes, Strawberry Jam Fritters, to name just a few of the delights that you can try for yourself. These traditional recipes from around Yorkshire will bring back the feel of the times and the series into your kitchen.

In Yorkshire they warmed the pot before making the tea, kettles were suspended above the hearth and

Claude Jeremiah was buying pigs at £11.10s.0d each from Joshua. It was also customary on a policeman's rural beat to accept a glass of wine and a piece of Christmas cake from several welcoming households.

Yorkshire's farmhouse kitchens always had hams hanging from the ceiling and the smell of freshly baked bread and oatcakes heavy in the air...
Oatcakes, bread and pies are still made in the old-fashioned way with love, care and devotion. The pie chapter in this book shows with what skill the cooks from the area have created the traditional steak and kidney pie, apple and pork pie, the beautiful marbled colours of the three-layer cheese pie, Yorkshire mint pasties and venison pasties that melt in your mouth.

The Glorious Twelfth brings game to the forefront of the cookery calendar and the chapter on game, gives you mouthwatering recipes for grouse, duckling, partridge, pheasant, rabbit, hare and venison.

Winter comes very quickly to *Heartbeat* country and Sergeant Blaketon's Winter Warmer and other recipes like Oxtail Soup with Fresh Tarragon Dumplings, Robin Hood Bay Crab Soup and Roast Sirloin of Beef with Herb Stuffing will certainly keep out the cold.

There is no other region in England that is so picturesque as the Yorkshire National Park when the snow is lightly covering its hills at Christmas. It is from here that PC Nick Rowan gives you his favourite Christmas feast with is very own Posh Nosh recipes.

The final chapter is on the food that keeps Yorkshire on the map of Europe. No one can compete with Yorkshire jams and preserves, and Yorkshire Relish, Rowan Jelly, Piccalilli and Rhubarb Chutney are the delicious accompaniments to the many Yorkshire dishes that are waiting to be discovered in the pages of this recipe book.

Tom Bridge — *Tom Bridge*

Chapter 1

The Yorkshire Pudding Story

Yorkshire without Yorkshire pudding, is very much like having
Heartbeat without the North Riding.

"*Take a quart of milk and five eggs, beat them*
well together, and mix them with flour till it is very smooth; put
in a little salt, some grated nutmeg and ginger; butter a dripping
or frying pan and put it under a piece of beef, mutton, or a
loin of veal that is roasting, and then put in your batter, and
when the top side is brown, cut it in square pieces, and turn it,
and then let the under side brown; then put it in a hot dish
*as clean of fat as you can, and send it to table hot.***"**

Hannah Glasse (Art of Cookery, 1796)

My Recipe for Perfect Yorkshire Pudding

The recipe today is made with milk and water to gain lightness and crispness. For a really crisp pudding, there must be no fat in the mixture. Other essentials for a good pudding are very hot fat coating the tin, and a good hot oven; gas mark 8, 230°C / 450°F. The pudding should be eaten with thick onion gravy as a separate course before the main meal, but nowadays it is more usual to serve it as an accompaniment to roast beef.

110g / 4oz plain flour (sifted)
½ tsp salt
1 large fresh egg
150 ml / 5 fl oz of fresh milk
150 ml / 5 fl oz of water
dripping or cooking fat

Sift the flour and salt into a large basin.

Break the egg into a saucer and then place it into the centre of the flour, adding enough milk and water to make a beating consistency with the whisk.

Beat well and leave to stand for 40 minutes.

Heat the oven to gas mark 7, 220°C / 425°F.

For small puddings, use 6 x 2.5cm bun tray and put 2 tablespoons of the batter into each individual pudding hole.

Bake for 15 to 20 minutes, or if making one large pudding, bake for 30 minutes, then cut the pudding into portions.

In some areas including the farms of East Riding, the Yorkshire pudding may be replaced by a suet pudding, which can be simply well seasoned, while others are filled with pork, bacon, sausage, steak, chicken or a variety of fillings which I have recreated for you, using the basic Yorkshire batter recipe on this page.

SERVES 4-6

Yorkshire Pudding with Mince and Onion

I do believe this recipe started its life using mutton, then a rabbit, but now I'm using beef, so really you can please yourself.

25g / 1oz dripping
225g / 8oz best minced beef
1 onion, finely chopped
seasoning
Yorkshire pudding batter (page10)

Pre-heat the oven to gas mark 7, 220°C / 425°F.

Heat the dripping in a large frying pan, add the minced beef and chopped onion and fry for 12 minutes.

Fill a large baking tray with some of the fat from the minced beef and place into the oven for 3 minutes until it is so hot that the fat is smoking.

Pour over the batter and sprinkle with the minced beef and onion.

Bake for 30 minutes and serve with a rich gravy.

SERVES 4

Corned Beef Pudding

If you had to travel to Rydale on a 1962 Francis Barnett motorbike when the snow is thick on the ground, I guarantee you would need a good helping of corned beef pudding to thaw you out.

350g / 12oz Corned beef, cut into small cubes
1 small onion, finely chopped
Yorkshire pudding batter

Pre-heat the ven to gas mark 7, 220°C / 425°F.

Fry the corned beef and onion in a little dripping for 3 minutes.

Place a large baking tray and the fat from the corned beef into the oven for 3 minutes until it is very hot, the fat should be smoking.

Pour over the batter and sprinkle with the corned beef and onion. Bake for 30 minutes and serve with a tomato sauce.(see page 138)

SERVES 4

Traditional Yorkshire Toad

The word 'toad' is synonymous with a quick and simple lunch or supper. If you don't like beef, try it with pork, lamb, poultry or game, ensuring that the meat is at least half-cooked before you bake it for the final 20 minutes.

25g / 1oz dripping
350g / 12oz chuck steak, trimmed of fat and cubed
salt
freshly milled black pepper
Yorkshire pudding batter (page 10)

Pre-heat the oven to gas mark 8, 230°C / 450°F

Heat the dripping in a baking tin until it is just smoking.

Pour in a quarter of the batter and bake for 10 minutes until the batter is just set. While the batter is baking, season the meat and lightly fry the meat until the batter is set, add the meat to the baking tin, pour in the remainder of the batter and return to the oven and bake for 20 minutes .

Lower the heat (without opening the oven) to 200°C / 400°F, gas mark 6 for 15 minutes.

And serve with a red wine sauce or onion gravy.

SERVES 4

Baked Herb Pudding

Use some fresh sage or mint to make this vegetarian supper dish. Traditionally, this was made with wild herbs from Northallerton, then served with mushy peas.

2 large onions, skinned, boiled and roughly chopped
1 tsp freshly chopped sage or mint
2 tbsp fresh white breadcrumbs
freshly milled black pepper
salt
Yorkshire pudding batter
1 tbsp vegetable oil

Pre-heat the oven to gas mark 4, 180°C / 350°F.

Into a large bowl, add the chopped onion, sage or mint, breadcrumbs, freshly milled black pepper and salt. Blend the dry mixture, then slowly blend in the batter, making sure the mixture is completly blended.

Heat the dripping in a large baking tin and pour over the batter mixture and bake in the centre of the oven for 40 minutes.

Seasoned Yorkshire Pudding with Pork

This recipe is far better if you use sweet apples and not cooking apples such as Bramleys.

25g / 1oz dripping
350g / 12oz pork fillet, cubed and seasoned
1 large onion, finely chopped
1 tbsp freshly chopped sage
Yorkshire pudding batter (page 10)
4 tbsp freshly chopped apple

Pre-heat the oven gas mark 7, 220°C / 425°F.

Heat the dripping in a large frying pan, add the seasoned pork, onion and sage, cook for 4 minutes.

Place the fat into the baking tray and place in the oven for 3 minutes until the fat is smoking.

Pour over the batter and sprinkle the pork, sage, onion and finally the apple pieces.

Bake for 30 minutes and serve with apple sauce (see page 139) and a glass of cider.

SERVES 4

Cooking Toad the Fowl Way

This really is a fowl recipe as it was originally used for preparing the wildfowl from the Yorkshire moors. The method was to boil the fowl until the meat dropped off the bones. The meat was served with Yorkshire pudding, and the bones and stock reserved for a nourishing soup.

1 tbsp dripping
275g / 10oz chicken breast meat, cut into thin strips
6 rashers streaky bacon, rindless, grilled and chopped
a pinch of nutmeg
freshly milled black pepper
Yorkshire pudding batter (page 10)

Pre-heat the oven to gas mark 7, 220°C / 425°F.

Heat the dripping in the baking tray, for 3 minutes until it is smoking. Season the chicken pieces with nutmeg and freshly milled black pepper.

Pour over the batter and scatter the chicken pieces and bacon around the baking tray. Bake for 30 minutes and serve with a white wine sauce.

SERVES 4

Baked Parsnip Pudding

If I were vegetarian, this would be my favourite dish. The sweetness of the parsnips complements the tarragon and, served with a creamy cheesy sauce, makes a brilliant supper dish. Young Gina makes this for Uncle George at the Aidensfield Arms from time to time. I think this should go permanently on the menu.

50g / 2oz dripping
450g / 16oz baby parsnips, peeled and cut into quarters
salt
15ml / 1 tbsp freshly chopped tarragon
Yorkshire pudding batter (page 000)

Pre-heat the Oven to gas mark 7, 220°C / 425°F.

Boil the parsnips in just enough salt water to cover them, for 4 minutes.

Strain them and dry them thoroughly.

Put the dripping into a baking tray and place in the oven until hot, add the parsnips and bake for 15 minutes.

Pour half the dripping into a small bowl and save. Add the batter, sprinkle with tarragon and bake for a further 30 minutes. Serve with a light cheese sauce.

SERVES 4-6

Ma Walsh's Fruity Fritters

Ma Walsh lives in Shipley and she is renowned for her Yorkshire fritter batter, but not until recently, would she give me this traditional and tasty recipe.

25g / 1oz dried yeast
150ml / 5 fl oz warm milk
225g / 8oz plain flour
50g / 2oz currants
50g / 2oz caster sugar
2 medium sized apples, cored, peeled and grated
25g / 1oz candied peel
a pinch freshly grated nutmeg
2 large eggs, whisked with a tablespoon of sherry
50g / 2oz beef dripping
25g / 1oz butter

Into a large bowl put the yeast and warm milk, whisk until it dissolves, then leave it to stand for a few minutes.

Sift the flour with all the other dry ingredients into another bowl. Add the eggs and blend. Slowly add enough milk to make a thick paste, sthen continue adding the milk to make a creamy batter.

Let the batter stand for at least 24 hours before using. Slowly whisk the batter.

Heat the dripping and butter in a large pan until it is hot, adding 1 tablespoon of the fritters at a time to the hot fat. Fry for 2 minutes either side until golden brown, drain onto some clean kitchen towel, sprinkle with sugar and serve them warm.

Chapter 2
Younger Than Springtime

All the traditional favourites come out in spring; bringing with them a taste from the past into the present. Naturally I have used the very best of British produce for all my recipes. After all, what is sweeter then home-reared lamb and home-grown vegetables and fruit?

CROWN OF ENGLISH LAMB

BEEF WELLY

ROAST LOIN OF ENGLISH
PORK

BREAST OF SPRING
LAMB IN HONEY WITH
MINT STUFFING

ROAST SIRLOIN OF ENGLISH
BEEF WITH YORKSHIRE
PUDDING

CORNED BEEF HASH

GREENGRASS'S
FARMHOUSE GRILL

DEVILLED CHICKEN

SHEPHERD'S PIE

LAMB'S LIVER WITH
YORKSHIRE RELISH

YORKSHIRE FISH 'N' CHIPS

CREAMED SPRINGTIME
VEGETABLE QUICHE

WENSLEYDALE APPLE CAKE

Crown of English Lamb

Yorkshire is a beautiful pastoral and agricultural region scattered with numerous hamlets and market towns. Lamb is in abundance and it is without doubt the most popular cut of meat in the area.

2 best end necks of lamb, with 6 cutlets, chinned on each
1 tbsp butter
1 onion, finely chopped
1 tsp freshly ground rosemary
1 eating apple, cored and chopped
1 pear, cored and chopped
100g / 4oz fresh breadcrumbs
2 tbsp freshly chopped mint
1 egg
salt
freshly milled black pepper
3 tbsp clear honey
400g / 1lb of black pudding, cut into slices 1cm / 1/2 inch thick

Pre-heat the oven to gas mark 4, 180°C / 350°F.

Trim each cutlet bone to a depth of 2.5cm / 1 inch with a sharp knife.

Bend the joints around, fat side inwards to form a crown.

Cover each exposed bone with cooking foil and place into a small baking tray.

Slowly melt the butter in a saucepan, add the onion, rosemary, apple and pear and cook for 4 minutes. Add the breadcrumbs, mint and egg, seasoning well.

Fill the centre of the crown with the stuffing. Cover the crown with cooking foil and bake for 80 minutes.

Ten minutes before the end of cooking time, remove the foil and pour the honey around the sides of the crown. Taking care not to touch the top of the crown, replace the foil and continue the cooking process.

Grill the black pudding for 3 minutes on either side.

Garnish with slices of grilled black pudding, fresh shallots glazed with the honey juices from the lamb and mint and onion gravy.(see page 138)

SERVES 4-6

Bccf Wclly

This is also known as Brontë pie; writing to her sister Emily from Brussels on 1st December, 1843, Charlotte mentioned how she would rather be in the kitchen at Haworth Parsonage, cutting up the hash, topping it with pastry and then baking it in the oven.

900g / 2lb beef fillet or sirloin
75g / 3oz butter
1 onion, finely chopped
175g / 6oz button mushrooms or wild mushrooms
450g / 1lb puff pastry (see page 91)
175g / 6oz chicken liver pâté
1 egg, lightly beaten
salt
freshly ground black pepper

With a sharp knife, trim the fat from the beef fillet or sirloin. Season the meat with salt and ground black pepper. Melt the butter in a large frying pan, add the beef, sealing the meat all over by cooking each side for at least 8 minutes. Remove the fillet from the pan, placing it to one side. In the same pan add a little more butter and add the chopped onion and mushrooms, cooking them until all the moisture has evaporated. Allow them to cool.

Pre-set the oven to gas 6, 200°C / 400°F.

Roll out the pastry into a large rectangle and place onto a greased baking sheet.

Spread the onion and mushroom mixture onto the centre of the pastry and place the beef onto the mixture. Top the fillet with a layer of pâté.

Brush the edges of the pastry with the beaten egg, fold and seal the pastry, by pressing in the edges.

Make some flowers and leaves from the left-over pastry and place them on the pastry-wrapped beef. Brush it completely with the beaten egg.

Bake in the centre of the oven for 20 minutes, then lower the oven to gas mark 4, 180°C / 350°F, for a further 15 minutes until golden brown.

SERVES 6-8

Author's tip: Should you not be a lover of red meat, try this recipe using turkey or chicken breast.

Roast Loin of English Pork

Yorkshire pigs can eat until they pop. Most are fed on left-over vegetable scraps. Nearly everyone in rural Yorkshire had a pig except me, so here's a delicious country recipe for pork with special emphasis on crunchy crackling!

2lb–6lb loin of pork
fresh rosemary
bay leaves
coarse salt
freshly ground black pepper
honey

Pre-heat the oven to Gas mark 8, 230°C / 450°F.

It is important that you adhere to the cooking time of 30 minutes per 450g / 1lb .

Score the loin of pork with a sharp knife.

To get the crackling really crisp, place the joint skin side down in a roasting tray and pour about 1 inch of boiling water over it.

Place the tray in the centre of the oven and cook for 20 minutes.

Remove the tray, pour off the liquid and use it for basting the pork.

Place the pork back into the roasting tin skin side up, season and add a few bay leaves and rosemary sprigs into the score marks.

Reduce the heat to gas mark 4, 180°C / 350°F and cook for 30 minutes per pound, basting every 20 minutes. Once cooked, allow to cool, remove the crackling, cut into long thin strips, place onto a baking tray, salt and coat with a little honey and cook for a further 10 minutes.

Garnish the plate with apple sauce (see page 139).

Lay the slices of pork and crackling into a fanned circle and serve hot or cold.

SERVES 4-6

Breast of Spring Lamb Baked in Honey with Mint Stuffing

The village of Aidensfield is surrounded by picturesque farmland, which in spring is covered with fleecy, white lambs. Only the plumpest of these should be used in this 1960's recipe.

900g / 2lb boned lamb breast
1 tsp ground ginger
2 tbsp of clear honey
30g / 1oz butter
1 onion, finely chopped
1 egg, beaten
2 tbsp port
100g / 4oz fresh breadcrumbs
4 tbsp finely chopped fresh mint
2 tbsp parsley chopped
salt
freshly ground black peppercorns

Melt the butter in a frying pan and fry the onion until soft.

In a separate bowl, beat the egg with the port and blend in the breadcrumbs, ginger, parsley and mint, add the onions and season the mixture with salt and freshly ground black pepper.

Flatten the meat and remove all the excess fat, place the mixture onto the meat, then roll up the meat tightly and secure it with some butchers' string.

Place the lamb onto a large piece of cooking foil. Warm the honey and pour over the lamb, securing the foil around the lamb so the honey or lamb juices do not escape.

Cook in a hot oven, gas mark 8, 230°C / 450°F for 35-40 minutes.

Very carefully remove the foil retaining the juices and place them into a saucepan.

Return the meat back to the oven for a further 15 minutes to brown.

Put some more finely chopped mint into the saucepan with the juice and add 15ml / 1 tbsp of port. Bring to the boil and let it simmer for 10 minutes, then strain the sauce through a fine sieve into a sauce boat and serve with the breast of lamb. Leave to rest for 10 minutes before carving.

SERVES 4-6

Roast Sirloin of English Beef with Yorkshire Pudding

This recipe is the pride and joy of Yorkshire! Dr Ferrenby recommends this to cure hunger pangs and confesses to a little medicinal gravy with his Yorkshires.

50g / 2oz beef dripping
1.4kg / 3lb beef sirloin
Yorkshire relish (see page 130)
Yorkshire Pudding Batter (see page10)

Pre-heat the oven to gas mark 4, 180°C / 350°F.

Put the beef into a shallow baking tin, season the meat well and pour over half the melted dripping.

Roast in the oven for 70 minutes.

Increase the oven temperature to 220°C / 425°F, gas mark 7. Put the rest of the dripping into a large baking tray and place in the oven for 3 minutes until the dripping is smoking.

Pour in the batter and bake for 30 minutes

Remove both the meat and Yorkshire pudding. Leave to rest for 10 minutes. Carve the beef, make a gravy with the juices and serve with Yorkshire pudding.

SERVES 4

Corned Bccf Hash

Easy and simple to make! Every Northern granny will have a similar recipe.

450g / 1lb tin of corned beef
1 large onion, roughly chopped
600ml / 1 pint of beef stock, thickened with a little cornstarch
1 tbsp mushroom ketchup
900g / 2lb mashed potatoes
50g / 2oz melted butter
75g / 3oz Cheddar cheese, grated
freshly ground black pepper

Pre-heat the oven to gas mark 4, 180°C / 350°F.

Chop the corned beef into half inch cubes, place into a casserole dish, top with the raw onion, sprinkle with the mushroom ketchup and cover with beef stock.

Top with the mashed potato, melted butter and grated cheese and season with freshly milled black pepper.

Bake for 20 to 25 minutes until golden brown.

SERVES 4

Greengrass's Farmhouse Grill

The healthy outdoor lifestyle on the Yorkshire moors will give you the heartiest of appetites. Greengrass's Farmhouse Grill is not for weight-watchers, but just the thing before, or after, a brisk six-hour walk.

4 lamb cutlets, trimmed
4 pork sausages
4 x 175g / 6oz rump steak
4 x 100g / 4oz gammon steak
2 lambs' or pigs' kidneys, cut in half
225g / 8oz button mushrooms
2 large beef tomatoes
salt
freshly milled black pepper
fresh watercress for garnish
4 pineapple rings or 4 poached eggs

Season all the meat with salt and freshly milled pepper and grill them until cooked – approximately 4 minutes on each side.

Place onto a large serving dish and keep them hot in a warm oven.

Add 2 tablespoons of cooking oil into a large frying pan and gently fry the mushrooms and tomatoes for 3 minutes.

Place them around the meat, garnish with some watercress, top the gammon steaks with a fresh pineapple ring or a poached egg.

SERVES 4

Devilled Chicken

A tasty spring dish which will bring the devil out in you.

350g / 12oz boneless chicken, skinned and diced
25g / 1oz plain flour
1 tbsp cayenne pepper
1 tsp paprika
25g / 1oz butter
1 onion, finely chopped
450ml / 15 fl oz milk
4 tbsp apple puree
100g / 4oz fresh grapes (white)
150ml / 5 fl oz soured cream.
sprinkle of paprika

Coat the chicken pieces in the flour, cayenne pepper and paprika, shaking off any excess flour or spice. Melt the butter in a saucepan and fry the chicken lightly with the chopped onion for 4 minutes.

Stir in the excess flour and spice, slowly blend in the milk, stirring until the sauce thickens. Let the chicken and sauce simmer until the sauce is smooth.

Add the apple puree and grapes and simmer gently for another 20 minutes.

Place the chicken and devilled sauce into a serving dish and top with soured cream and a sprinkle of paprika.

SERVES 4

Shepherd's Pie

By hook or crook, you will enjoy this!

450g / 1lb lean minced lamb
1 large onion, skinned and finely chopped
2 carrots, peeled and finely diced
25g / 1oz plain flour
300ml / 10 fl oz lamb stock (a cube will do)
1 tbsp tomato puree
salt
freshly milled black pepper
a pinch of fresh thyme
900g / 2lb creamed potatoes
75g / 3oz Wensleydale cheese, grated

Pre-heat the oven to gas mark 6, 200°C / 400°F.

Dry fry the minced lamb in a non-stick saucepan, adding the onion and diced carrots. Cook for 12 minutes.

Sprinkle the lamb with flour and heat for a further 3 minutes. Slowly blend in the stock and tomato puree, simmer for 20 minutes, seasoning with salt, pepper and thyme.

Put the lamb into an oven proof casserole and allow the meat to cool.

Top the minced lamb with the mashed potato and sprinkle with the cheese. Bake in the oven for 25 minutes and serve with freshly minted green peas.

SERVES 4

Lamb's Liver with Yorkshire Relish

Yorkshire folk don't like their food covered in fancy sauces! It makes them think the food's hidden because there's something wrong with it. However a compromise can be reached by serving the meat with Yorkshire relish.

450lb / 16oz lamb's liver, thinly sliced
salt
freshly milled black pepper
25g / 1oz plain flour
25g / 1oz cooking oil
25g / 1oz dripping
12 shallots, peeled
1 clove garlic, crushed
150ml /5 fl oz rich gravy
150ml / 5 fl oz Yorkshire Relish (see page 130)

Dust the liver with salt and seasoned flour.

Heat the oil and dripping and fry the liver quickly on both sides so that the liver remains pink inside. Remove the liver from the pan and keep it warm.

Add the shallots, garlic and gravy to the pan and simmer for 5 minutes. Add the Yorkshire relish and simmer for a further 10 minutes. Return the liver and the juices back to the pan and simmer for a further 5 minutes.

Arrange slices of the liver and shallots onto individual warm plates, strain the sauce through a non-metallic sieve and pour over the liver.

Serve with new potatoes and button mushrooms.

SERVES 4

Fish 'n' Chips

From Scarborough, Whitby and Bridlington come the famous haddock which goes into every fish and chip shop in every town and village across Yorkshire. The recipe below is truly unique due to the addition of beer into the batter mix.

4 x 225g / 8oz cod or haddock fillets
1 kg / 2½lb potatoes, peeled and chipped
dripping or sunflower cooking oil
salt
freshly ground white pepper

Batter mixture
200g / 7oz plain flour
1 egg whisked with 2 tbsp beer
salt
150ml / 5 fl oz milk and water mixed
freshly milled white pepper

To make the batter, mix the flour, egg, milk and seasoning until the batter is very smooth and lump free. Leave it to stand for at least 1 hour.

Heat the oil until it gives off a faint blue smoke (180°C / 350°F). Fry the chips in small batches and when they start to brown remove them with a small slotted spoon. Place them into a warm oven.

Season each piece of fish, then dip into the batter, drawing it backwards and forwards 2 to 3 times to coat the fish fully. Lower it gently into the hot fat, with skin side down to prevent the fish from curling.

Fry them one at a time. After 5 minutes turn the fish over, cooking until brown for a further 3 minutes.

Traditionally they should be served on newspaper with salt and malt vinegar.

Springtime Creamed Vegetable Quiche

A selection of springtime produce from the gardens of the Dales makes this a meal to remember.

350g / 12oz shortcrust pastry (see page 91)
25g / 1oz butter
100g / 4oz spring onions, chopped
100g / 4oz leeks, white end, washed and shredded
100g / 4oz button mushrooms, sliced
100g / 4oz fresh sweet peas
salt
freshly milled black pepper
175g / 6oz Wensleydale cheese, grated
2 whole eggs
1 egg yolk
150ml / 5 fl oz milk
150ml / 5 fl oz double cream mixed

Pre-heat the oven to gas mark 5, 190°C / 375°F.

Roll out the pastry and line a 25cm / 10 inch fluted flan/cake tin with a removable base.

Melt the butter in a large frying pan and fry the onions, leeks, mushrooms and peas over a low heat for 6 minutes.

Remove from the heat, sprinkle the base with half of the cheese, then layer with the remaining vegetables and top with the remaining cheese.

Beat the eggs, milk and cream and pour carefully over the vegetables and cheese.

Bake in the centre of the oven for 35 to 45 minutes until the vegetable quiche is set and golden brown.

Serve with a hot selection of seasonal vegetables to enhance this vegetarian delight.

SERVES 4-6

Wensleydale Apple Cake

A 1960s recipe containing the flavour of Yorkshire's finest cheese.

250g / 9oz self-raising flour
100g / 4oz caster sugar
175g / 6oz butter
1 egg, beaten
500m / 2 fl oz fresh milk
4 apples, peeled, cored and sliced
50g / 2oz sultanas
150g / 5oz Wensleydale cheese, grated
freshly grated nutmeg
1 tbsp lemon juice
2 tbsp clear honey
1 tbsp roasted almond niblets
150ml / 5 fl oz whipped double cream

Pre-heat the oven gas mark 6, 200°C / 400°F

Grease and line a 20.5cm / 8 inch cake tin with greaseproof paper.

Sift the flour and half the sugar into a bowl. Add 100g / 4oz of the butter, lightly blending the mixture with your fingertips until it resembles breadcrumbs. Add the egg and milk and mix to a soft texture.

Place the mixture into the cake tin, placing half the apple slices on top together with the sultanas. Top with the grated cheese.

Finish off with the remaining apples, sprinkle with sugar and little pieces of butter and the lemon juice.

Bake in the centre of the oven for 40-45 minutes.

Remove carefully from the oven, allow it to cool and place the cake onto a large plate. Pour over a little clear honey, top with roasted almond niblets and serve with double cream.

SERVES 6

Chapter 3

A Heartbeat Picnic

The Great British Picnic is an old established tradition, and nowhere does the national passion for picnicking show itself more clearly than in Yorkshire. At weekends and bank holidays people flock to the North Yorkshire Moors to drink in the beauty of the countryside and feast upon a lavish spread carefully prepared at home. Beckhole, near Goathland (Aidensfield in Heartbeat) has always been one of the most popular picnic spots in the region. Indeed recent episodes of Heartbeat must bring back some happy memories for some sixties' picnickers! In this section I choose a varied selection of cheeses from around the Yorkshire area, together with a choice of favourite breads, salads, cakes and fruit. All these delicious dishes can be washed down with Father O'Malley's home-made ginger beer or lemonade.

RANDYMERE SPICED BREAD
(WITH CHEESE)

NORTHALLERTON APPLE
CAKE (WITH CHEESE)

EGG, BACON AND SAUSAGE
CRISS CROSS

FATHER O'MALLEY'S
GINGER BEER

OPEN MOCK CRAB
SANDWICHES OR WHITBY
CRAB SANDWICHES

LAMB'S LIVER PÂTÉ

CHICKEN AND MUSHROOM
TART

KNARESBOROUGH PICNIC PIE

POTTED SMOKED TROUT

YORKSHIRE CURD TARTS

MOGGY

BRANDY SNAPS

LEMONADE

SUMMER DRINK

SUMMER SALADS

Randymere Spiced Bread (with cheese)

This is the bread folk make all the time in Rowan, Yorkshire – it's so delicious we can never eat enough of it!

1lb plain flour
a pinch of salt
10g / half tsp dried yeast
1 tsp sugar
1 egg, beaten
450ml / 15 fl oz warm milk
225g / 8oz mixed dried fruit
25g / 1oz candied peel
150g / 5oz sugar
2 tsp mixed spice
50g butter to line two non-stick bread tins
450g / 1lb Wensleydale cheese

Pre-heat the oven to gas mark 8, 230°C / 450°F.

Put the flour and a pinch of salt into a large clean bowl.

Cream the yeast together with the teaspoonful of sugar and the beaten egg, mixing them thoroughly. Add the yeast mixture to the warmed milk. Add the mixture to the flour, again mixing well.

Cover the bowl with a slightly dampened cloth and leave in a warm place for 1 hour.

Turn out the dough and knead, working in the fruit, peel, sugar and spices.

Cut the mixture in half and place the dough into two buttered tins. Cover again and leave in a warm place for a further 30 minutes. Bake in the oven for 10 minutes, then reduce the heat to Gas mark 4, 180°C / 350°F for 40 minutes.

Place the bread on a wire rack, allow to cool, slice and butter and serve with Wensleydale cheese and seedless grapes.

SERVES 6-8

Northallerton Apple Cake (with cheese)

This apple cake is traditionally served with cheese and beer in the pubs around Northallerton.

50g / 2oz Demerara sugar
4 tbsp golden syrup
75g / 3oz butter
175g / 6oz self-raising flour
1 tsp ground ginger
1 egg, whisked
225g / 8oz cooked apple puree

Pre-heat the oven to gas mark 5, 190°C / 375°F.

Melt the butter with the syrup and sugar for 3 minutes, then allow to cool.

Sift the flour with the ginger, add the egg, syrup mixture and apple puree, beating them together with a whisk.

Place the mixture into buttered baking tins and bake for 30 minutes.

Served with goats cheese and a good beer, this is wonderful.

SERVES 6-8

Egg, Bacon and Sausage Criss Cross

This is a very tasty picnic dish which can be served hot for tea. Cold, at a picnic, it's wonderful with home-made ginger beer.

350g / 12oz ready-made shortcrust pastry
3 large hard-boiled eggs, shelled
8 lean rashers of rindless streaky bacon, grilled
225g / 8oz sausage meat
1 egg beaten
150ml / 5 fl oz milk
salt
freshly milled black pepper

Pre-heat the oven to gas mark 6, 200°C / 400°F.

Roll out two thirds of the pastry and line a buttered pie dish or deep plate with it. Slice the eggs and chop the bacon and place those ingredients with small pieces of the sausage meat around the pastry case. Pour the egg and milk mixture over them.

Season well then roll out the remaining pastry and cut into thin strips of about half an inch and lay them across the pie to make a criss cross pattern, sealing the edges.

Bake in the centre of the oven for 10 minutes, then reduce the heat to gas mark 4, 180°C / 350°F for a further 25 minutes.

SERVES 6

Father O'Malley's Ginger Beer

Good for the soul!

450g / 1lb sugar
Juice of 2 lemons
1 tbsp cream of tartar
75g / 3oz fresh root ginger, peeled and mashed
2 litres of boiling water
1 egg white

Put the sugar, juice from the lemons, cream of tartar and the ginger into a very large bowl. Pour over the boiling water and then stir in the egg white, which will clarify the ginger beer. Let the liquid stand for 24 hours.

Stir the ginger beer, then strain through a fine non-metallic sieve. Bottle and allow the ginger beer to stand in a cool dark area for 4 days before drinking. This helps to improve the flavour.

SERVES 14

Whitby Crab Sandwiches
or Open Mock Crab Sandwiches

If you're not lucky enough to enjoy fresh crabs from Robin Hood's Bay, mock crab will make a delicious alternative. Use thickly sliced bread or French bread.

6 thick slices of bread (crusts removed) or a large french stick, buttered, cut lengthways then cut into 6 segments.
3 hard-boiled eggs, the yolk sieved and white chopped
25g / 1oz softened butter
2 tbsp prepared English mustard
1 tsp anchovy essence
freshly milled black pepper
200g / 8oz Wensleydale cheese, grated
3 cooked chicken breasts, skinned and finely chopped
12 slices of tomato and cucumber

Reserve the yolk and white from one egg.

Mix the ingredients with the butter, mustard and anchovy essence and season well with the freshly ground black pepper and spread the mixture onto the bread.

Lay the egg yolk and white on the top of the spread, then line with tomato and cucumber through the centre. Garnish with cress.

For the Whitby Crab Sandwiches use 450g / 1lb white and brown fresh crab meat instead of the cheese and chicken.

SERVES 6

Lamb's Liver Pâté

This recipe is on several menus in restaurants and hotels throughout Yorkshire, served with crusty bread and a glass of Yorkshire bitter.

175g / 6oz butter
500g / 1lb lamb's liver, finely chopped
275g / 10oz streaky bacon, rindless, finely chopped
1 large onion, finely chopped
a pinch of nutmeg
salt
freshly milled black pepper
4 tbsp brandy

Melt 150g / 5oz of the butter in a large frying pan or skillet, add the finely chopped liver, bacon and onion, simmer gently for 20 minutes, seasoning with a little nutmeg, salt and freshly milled black pepper. Take off the heat.

At the last minute add the brandy, whisking well with the liver paste. Turn the mixture into a small loaf tin. Melt the remaining butter and pour over the top of the pâté to seal the surface.

Chill in the refrigerator for two hours. Take the pâté to your picnic with a large french stick and serve with a glass of cold Yorkshire bitter.

SERVES 8

Chicken and Mushroom Tart

This lovely tart is just as delicious hot or cold.

350g / 12oz ready made shortcrust pastry
25g / 1oz butter
1 onion, finely chopped
75g / 3oz button mushrooms, finely chopped
25g / 1oz plain flour
2 eggs combined with 300ml / 10 fl oz milk
225g / 8oz cooked chicken breast, diced
salt
freshly milled black pepper
75g / 3oz Wensleydale cheese, grated

Pre-heat the oven to gas mark 7, 220°C / 425°F.

Roll out the pastry on a floured surface and line a round baking tray or deep plate. Bake blind in the oven for 5 minutes, then allow the pastry to cool.

Melt the butter in a frying pan, add the onions and mushrooms and cook for 2 minutes. Add the flour, turn the heat down very low and slowly add the milk. Sprinkle the chicken meat into the mixture and season well with salt and freshly milled pepper.

Remove from the heat and allow to cool. Pour the cooled mixture into the pastry case, sprinkle with the cheese and cook in the oven for 20 minutes at gas mark 4, 180°C / 350°F.

SERVES 6 TO 8

Knaresborough Picnic Pie

What a pie! This is the forerunner to the established ham and egg pie, and it's much better. Start with a layer of York ham, follow it with a layer of raw eggs and then grated cheese. Repeat the process; once the pie has been cooked I promise you'll be in a Yorkshire heaven!

350g / 12oz shortcrust pastry (see page 91)
450g / 16oz York ham, thinly sliced
12 eggs
225g / 8oz Swaledale or Wensleydale cheese, grated
salt
freshly milled black pepper
1 egg and a little milk to coat the pastry lid

Pre-heat the oven to gas mark 5, 190°C / 375°F.

Roll out two thirds of the pastry and grease and line a deep pie dish.

Layer with slices of ham, raw eggs and cheese, seasoning each layer with salt and freshly ground black pepper. Finish with a layer of York ham.

Cover the pie with a pastry lid, seal with a little egg and milk mixture and bake in the oven for 25 minutes.

SERVES 6

Potted Smoked Trout

Quick and simple, this is one of those recipes you can make using any type of smoked fish. Like many in the North Riding, PC Rowan fishes for trout in season.

350g / 12oz smoked trout fillets
freshly milled black pepper
2 tbsp English mustard
175g / 6oz unsalted butter, softened
juice of ½ lemon

Remove the skin from the trout fillets, place them in a blender or pound them into small flakey pieces in a bowl.

Add the mustard and softened butter, blending again until the whole mixture is very smooth and add the lemon juice. Mix well. Serve chilled with fresh brown bread and butter.

SERVES 8-10

Yorkshire Curd Tarts

This is the 1960's Yorkshire version of today's cheesecake.

Pastry
100g / 4oz butter, diced
225g / 8oz plain flour
25g / 1oz caster sugar
1 egg yolk, whisked with 3 tbsp water

Filling
225g / 8oz curd cheese
50g / 2oz currants
75g / 3oz caster sugar
2 eggs, beaten
finely grated rind of 1 lemon
a pinch of nutmeg

Pre-heat the oven to gas mark 4, 180°C / 350°F.

To make the pastry, place the butter and flour into a clean bowl and rub the mixture until it resembles fine breadcrumbs. Add 25g / 1oz of the sugar, then mix in the egg yolk and water to make a firm dough.

Knead the dough lightly, then roll it out on a floured surface. Line the greased individual patty tins.

To make the filling, mash the cheese with the remaining sugar, currants, eggs, lemon rind and nutmeg, thoroughly blending all the ingredients together.

Spoon the mixture into the pastry cases. Grate over a little more nutmeg. Bake in the centre of the oven for 25 to 30 minutes until the pastry is brown and the filling set.

SERVES 12

Moggy

Moggy is a traditional Yorkshire scone. The name has been taken from the Norse language, where a pile of corn was a Mugi. It's a dream at picnics, buttered then spread with dollops of home-made strawberry jam (see page 130).

450g / 1lb plain flour
a pinch of salt
2 tsp baking powder
100g / 4oz butter, softened
100g / 4oz lard, softened
175g / 6oz golden syrup
175g / 6oz caster sugar
150ml / 5 fl oz milk

Pre-heat the oven to gas mark 4, 180°C / 350°F.

Sift the flour, salt and baking powder into a clean mixing bowl. Rub in the softened butter and lard to form a breadcrumb base.

Add the syrup and sugar, mixing thoroughly. Add the milk to form a stiff dough. With your hand gently flatten to about 2 inches in thickness, and cut into triangle shape scones.

Grease a baking tray with a little butter, place the moggies onto the tray and bake them for 25 minutes until they are firm and lightly browned.

SERVES 6

Brandy Snaps

These biscuits have been connected with Yorkshire for centuries. They're ideal at picnics on the Moors, served with lightly whipped cream and freshly picked strawberries. If they last more than one feast, they should be stored in an airtight container !

50g / 2oz butter
50g / 2oz caster sugar
2 tbsp golden syrup
50g / 2oz plain flour
1 tsp ground ginger
1 tsp brandy

Pre-heat the oven to gas mark 4, 180°C / 350°F.

Slowly melt the butter, sugar and syrup in a saucepan, then remove the saucepan from the heat.

Sift the flour and ginger together, then add to the melted butter mixture, stirring in the lemon rind. Mix thoroughly.

Line a greased baking tray with grease-proof paper and drop teaspoons of the mixture onto the baking sheet, leaving 10cm (4 inches) between them.

Bake in the oven for about 7 minutes or until they are light brown and set.

Allow them to cool on the sheet for 2 minutes, then loosen them with a palette knife.

Remove and roll each one around the buttered handle of a wooden spoon. Leave them on the handle to set, gently twisting to remove them and allow them to cool on a wire rack.

When they have cooled and set, place them into an airtight container.

Fill them with cream when required and serve them with fresh strawberries and an ice-cold glass of Yorkshire Loving Cup.

SERVES 6

Traditional Yorkshire Lemonade

There is no comparison between the bottled gassy lemonade you buy in the shops and and the smell and taste of home-made lemonade. This is ideal for picnics and outdoor summer parties.

8 large lemons
200g / 8oz granulated sugar
2 litres of boiling water

Wash and peel the lemons. Cut the lemon into half and remove any white pith from the strips of zest with a sharp knife. This prevents the lemonade from tasting bitter.

Put the zest and the lemons and their juice into a large bowl . Add the sugar and pour over 2 litres of boiling water. Stir and cover with a clean dry towel and allow the lemonade to stand for 24 hours. Stir again then strain through a non-metallic sieve. Check for sweetness and add a little more sugar should you wish to do so. Should the lemonade be to strong, dilute it with some more water.

Pour the lemonade into large serving jugs with plenty of ice. If you are taking the lemonade on a picnic, put ice into a large flask, pour in the lemonade and tighten the flask top.

SERVES ABOUT 14

OTHER SUMMER DRINKS

Yorkshire Loving Cup

There is plenty of romance to be found in Yorkshire and champagne does occasionally flow in the heat of the summer, so why not try this soothing ice-cold romantic drink.

2 lemons, peeled and thinly sliced
4 tsp sugar
6 lemon balm leaves or spearmint leaves
600ml / 20 fl oz cold water
300ml / 10 fl oz Madeira wine
150ml / 5 fl oz cognac
1 bottle of ice-cold champagne

Place all the ingredients except the champagne into a large jug, stir and chill for 2 hours.

Just before serving, add the bottle of champagne and serve with fresh brandy snaps (see page 36) and strawberries.

SERVES 14 DRINKS

Strawberry Cream and Champagne Surprise

This is one of the most delightful drinks; it's so easy to make and yet everyone will ask what is in it. You can taste the strawberries and cream but not the Cointreau, which gives this summer cocktail its unique flavour.

225g / 8oz fresh strawberries, washed and hulled
4 tbsp Bols Strawberry Liqueur
2 tbsp Cointreau
150ml / 5 fl oz double cream
crushed ice
1 bottle of champagne
8 strawberries

Blend the strawberries, Bols, Cointreau and lemon juice in a blender until liquidized. Add the cream and blend for 10 seconds.

Pour the strawberry and cream juice into a large jug. Chill for 1 hour, top with crushed ice and strawberries, pour in the champagne and serve.

SERVES 8

SUMMER SALAD DAYS

I have put together four simple salads to go with all the recipes in this section, plus Nick Rowan's Heartbeat country salad dressing and my classic mayonnaise to show you how easy it is to make them for yourself.

Crispy Roast Duck and Bacon Salad

225g / 8oz cold, crispy roast duck meat, skin removed
225g / 8oz rindless streaky bacon, grilled until crispy
3 tbsp olive oil
1 tbsp white wine vinegar
salt
freshly milled black pepper
50g / 2oz cashew nuts
4 sticks celery, chopped
1 large dessert apple, cored and diced
1 large beetroot, cooked and diced
4 tbsp mayonnaise (see page 39)
2 tbsp freshly chopped chives
1 crisp lettuce
2 oranges, sliced into segments
2 beef tomatoes, sliced

Slice the cooked duck meat and bacon into bite size pieces and gently fry in the olive oil for a few minutes. Remove from the heat and add the wine vinegar. Season the duck and bacon with a little salt and plenty of freshly milled black pepper.

Place the duck and bacon into a large bowl and toss in all the other ingredients except the lettuce, orange segments and tomato.

Decorate a plate with lettuce, add the duck and bacon mixture into the centre of it and garnish with orange segments and slices of beef tomatoes.

Nick's Fab Salad

Even policemen sometimes have a day off and Nick's known to be a bit of a dab hand in the kitchen!

450g / 1lb cooked potatoes, diced
1 tbsp lime juice
8 frankfurter sausages, cooked and chopped
225g / 8oz cooked chicken breast, chopped
2 large beetroots, cooked, peeled and diced
4 spring onions, peeled and chopped
150ml / 5 fl oz mayonnaise (see page 39)
freshly ground black pepper

Garnish
crisp lettuce leaves
fresh mustard cress
2 limes sliced
2 beef tomatoes sliced

Carefully blend all the ingredients together and chill for 1 hour, then place the mixture onto a bed of crisp lettuce leaves, garnished with mustard cress, sliced limes and sliced beef tomatoes.

SERVES 4

Sixties Salad Days

*Salads have been popular since the 1860's
in Yorkshire and this recipe dates from then.
This is a good salad to stuff into baked potatoes
for a filling lunch.*

*1 small red cabbage shredded
1 large onion, peeled and sliced
2 carrots, peeled and grated
75g / 3oz currants
1 tbsp warmed honey
150ml / 5 fl oz mayonnaise (see below)
1 tsp curry paste
freshly milled black pepper
4 jacket potatoes (hot)
2 tbsp freshly snipped chives*

Place the cabbage, onion, carrots and currants into
large salad bowl and toss. In a separate bowl, blend
the slightly warmed honey, mayonnaise, curry paste
and freshly milled black pepper. Put the vegetable
ingedients in with the mayonnaise and mix. Serve
inside the hot jacket potatoes.

Heartbeat Country Dressing Style Salads

*1 tsp of salt
1 tsp dry English mustard
1 tsp sugar
1 tsp freshly milled black pepper
1 clove of garlic crushed
6 tbsp white wine vinegar
150ml / 5 fl oz olive oil*

Place all the ingredients into a screwtop jar. Chill for
1 hour before serving. Shake the jar well to mix the
ingredients. This dressing will keep for at least 3
months if the screwtop is kept tightly shut.

MAKES APPROX 220ML.

Wensleydale Cheese Salad

*275g / 10oz Wensleydale cheese, diced
4 sticks of celery, chopped
1 red dessert apple, cored and chopped
1 large carrot, peeled and roughly grated
50g / 2oz walnuts, chopped
100g / 4oz sultanas
3 tbsp sesame oil
12 stuffed olives in brine and 1 tbsp of the juice
100g / 4oz seedless grapes, cut into halves*

Toss all the ingredients into a large salad bowl and
chill for 1 hour.

Quick Classic Mayonnaise

*6 egg yolks
1 tsp ready-made English mustard
a pinch of salt
freshly milled black pepper
1 tbsp lemon juice
600ml / 20 fl oz olive oil
1 tbsp boiling water*

Place the egg yolks, mustard, salt, ground pepper
and lemon juice into a large clean bowl. Beat them
together with a hand whisk, electric mixer or
blender. Slowly add the oil, drop by drop, to the egg
mixture whisking very briskly all the time.

Then add the oil a little quicker, in a thin but
steady stream as the mayonnaise begins to thicken.
Add the boiling water and transfer the mayonnaise
to a jar.

For a garlic mayonnaise add 2 tablespoons of
crushed garlic at the beginning with the lemon juice
and continue as before.

For a herb mayonnaise add 3 tablespoons of your
favourite fresh herbs once you have made the
mayonnaise.

MAKES APPROX 600ML / 20 FL OZ

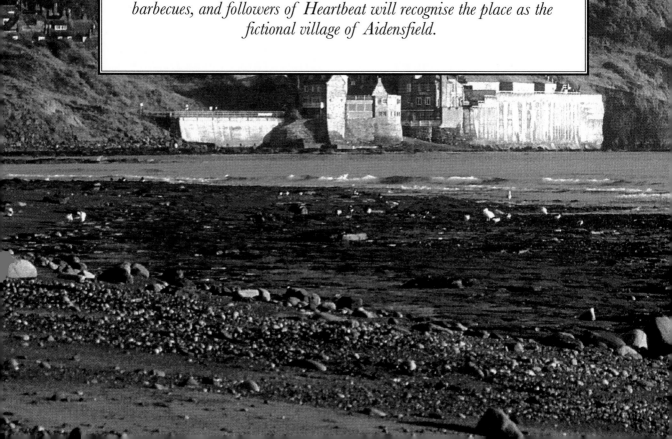

Chapter 4

A Summer Barbecue

Barbecues are far less formal affairs than dinner parties. Very often, they give the hostess a chance to relax and have a few drinks while the host busies himself over the glowing embers. Again, as with picnics, barbecues give everyone the opportunity to eat 'al fresco' and are the perfect way to spend a long summer's evening. Rather than having a barbecue in your back garden, you can visit a barbecue area with your friends. Osmotherly, Hutton-le-Hole, Billdale, Stokesley and Hemsley are just a few areas within Yorkshire which have their own barbecue sites. Goathland is another popular place for barbecues, and followers of Heartbeat will recognise the place as the fictional village of Aidensfield.

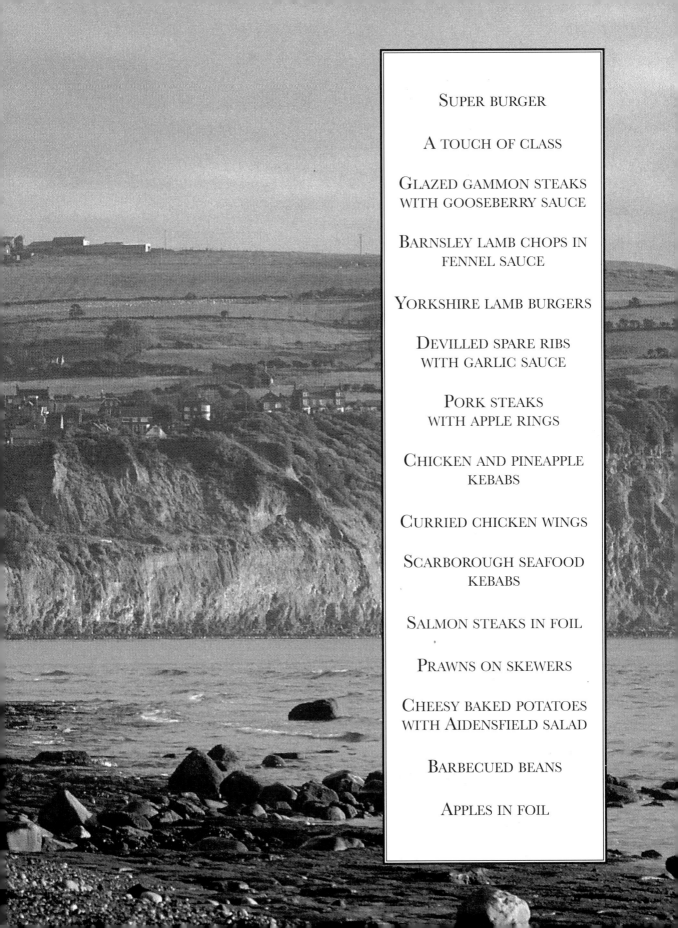

SUPER BURGER

A TOUCH OF CLASS

GLAZED GAMMON STEAKS
WITH GOOSEBERRY SAUCE

BARNSLEY LAMB CHOPS IN
FENNEL SAUCE

YORKSHIRE LAMB BURGERS

DEVILLED SPARE RIBS
WITH GARLIC SAUCE

PORK STEAKS
WITH APPLE RINGS

CHICKEN AND PINEAPPLE
KEBABS

CURRIED CHICKEN WINGS

SCARBOROUGH SEAFOOD
KEBABS

SALMON STEAKS IN FOIL

PRAWNS ON SKEWERS

CHEESY BAKED POTATOES
WITH AIDENSFIELD SALAD

BARBECUED BEANS

APPLES IN FOIL

Super Burger

This is a whopping double lamb and beef burger served with jacket potatoes and soured cream, roast corn on the cob, garlic bread and a cooling glass of Yorkshire iced tea.

Burgers
600g / 20oz minced lamb
600 / 20oz minced beef
3 large onions, finely chopped
100g / 4oz fresh breadcrumbs
2 tbsp Worcestershire sauce

Filling
4 large burger buns
4 slices of Wensleydale cheese
4 tbsp English mustard

Mix the minced lamb with 1 chopped onion, 50g / 2oz fresh breadcrumbs and 1 teaspoon of Worcestershire sauce.

Repeat the same process with the minced beef and shape into burgers.

Grill the burgers for 10 minutes or until they are cooked, fry the onions and toast the buns on the barbecue.

Place the bottom of each bun onto a serving plate. Put some cooked onion on the bottom of each bun, followed by the lamburger, a slice of cheese, some English mustard, a beefburger, mayonnaise, shredded lettuce and tomato slices, then top this off with the other half of the burger bun.

SERVES 4

A Touch of Class

A classy touch to any barbecue. This recipe is a bit pricy but it's worth every pound, shilling and penny.

900g / 2 lb beef fillet
100g / 4oz rough pâté
2 tbsp chopped chives
greased cooking foil
salt
freshly milled black pepper
50g / 2oz melted butter
150ml / 5 fl oz brandy

Slice the beef fillet down the centre and place the pâté and chives in it. Fold the fillet over to ensure the filling does not come out.

Place the fillet onto a large piece of cooking foil, season the steak well with salt and freshly milled black pepper.

Pour over the butter and half the brandy, then wrap and seal the beef fillet in the foil. Cook over the barbecue for 12 minutes.

Remove the foil, reserving the juices. Place onto the barbecue and grill until cooked, basting with the juices and remainder of the brandy. Be very careful when doing this and make sure children are not standing close.

Slice and serve with garlic bread

Glazed Gammon Steaks with Gooseberry Sauce

The finest ham in the world is York ham and there is no better way to serve it than with a rich gooseberry sauce.

4 x 275g / 10oz York Gammon Steaks, trimmed
4 tbsp apricot jam

Sauce
1kg / 2 lb gooseberries, topped and tailed
300ml / 10 fl oz sweet cider
250g / 8oz brown sugar
25g / 1oz ground allspice

Trim the gammon, making 1.5cm / ½ inch cuts at 2.5cm / 1 inch intervals along the fatty edge to stop the gammon from curling.

Place the gammon steaks onto the barbecue and grill for 8 minutes on either side, coating with the apricot jam for the last minute on either side.

Meanwhile, put the gooseberries and cider into a saucepan and bring to the boil. Simmer for 15 minutes then add the sugar and allspice and cook for a further 5 minutes.

Place the gammon steaks onto a serving dish, and generously coat each steak with the gooseberry sauce.

Serve with corn on the cob and a lightly coated potato salad.

SERVES 4

Barnsley Lamb Chops in Fennel Sauce

This sauce acts initially as a marinade. Later it can be reheated and served as a sauce to accompany the chops. Served with barbecued new potatoes and braised celery, these chops will melt in your mouth.

4 x 275g / 10oz Barnsley chops, trimmed

Marinade
150ml / 5 fl oz olive oil
2 tsp lemon juice
1 tbsp white wine vinegar
large onion, chopped
1 tsp fennel seed, crushed
salt
freshly milled black pepper
2 tbsp of port

Mix all the ingredients together in a bowl and leave the mixture to stand for 2 hours.

Completely cover the chops with the marinade and chill for a further 2 hours.

Barbecue the chops for approximately 5 minutes on either side.

SERVES 4

Yorkshire Lamb Burgers

From Goathland to Hutton-le-Hole, Rievaulx to Castleton, Danby and Egton, the old North Riding is sheep – and lamb – country. Here's a special barbecue recipe to celebrate good Yorkshire lamb at its best.

8 spring onions, finely chopped
1 cooking apple, cored and finely chopped
2 tbsp dripping
450g / 1 lb lean minced lamb
75g / 3oz breadcrumbs
1 tsp crushed rosemary
1 tbsp tomato ketchup
salt
freshly ground black pepper

Fry the spring onions and cooking apple in the dripping for 3 minutes.

Remove from the heat. Allow to cool and blend thoroughly with all the remaining ingredients. Shape the lamb mixture into four burgers and grill on the barbecue for 7 minutes on each side.

SERVES 4

Devilled Spare Ribs with Garlic Sauce

In most Yorkshire cottages and farmhouses, folk cure their own hams and throw the ribs to their dogs. However, ribs are also popular for barbecues and, served with this garlic sauce, they will keep the devil at bay.

2kg / 4lb pork ribs cut into 7.5cm / 3 inches in length

Marinade
3 tbsp crushed garlic
120ml / 4 fl oz soy sauce
120ml / 4 fl oz sweet cider
4 tbsp finely chopped spring onions
1 tsp crushed fennel seed
1 tbsp tomato puree
2 tbsp of clear honey
freshly milled black pepper
1 tbsp of cornflour mixed with 2 tbsp dry sherry
5 tbsp soured cream or yoghurt

Combine all the marinade ingredients except the cornflour paste and soured cream.

Coat the ribs and let them marinade for 24 hours.

Remove the ribs from the marinade and place them on the barbecue. Cook for 5 minutes on either side.

Place the marinade into a saucepan, bring to the boil and simmer for 4 minutes. Add the cornflour paste and soured cream, simmer for a further 3 minutes to make a thick creamy garlic sauce to serve with the ribs.

Try these ribs with warm bread to dip into the sauce. Have a sprig of fresh parsley at hand to get rid of the smell of garlic from your breath.

Simply wash the parsley in cold water and chew it for 2 minutes.

SERVES 8

Pork Steaks with Apple Rings

The combination of flavours from the mustard, bacon, brown sugar and apple is truly mouthwatering. However, barbecues are all about experimentation, so add a few of your own flavours like herbs or a pineapple ring instead of apple and garnish the steaks with slices of mango or kiwi fruit. Whatever you decide, try to enjoy yourself...

4 x 275g / 10oz pork steaks, edges trimmed
salt
freshly milled black pepper
4 tbsp English or Dijon mustard
4 apple rings
50g / 2oz soft brown sugar
8 large rashers of rindless streaky smoked bacon
salt
freshly milled black pepper
sweet cider

Season the steaks and barbecue them for 3 minutes on either side. Remove them and allow them to cool.

Coat them with mustard, top with a ring of apple, sprinkle with some soft brown sugar, wrap them in bacon and season again with salt and freshly milled black pepper and grill apple side down on the barbecue for 3 minutes either side. Sprinkle with a little sweet cider during the cooking process.

Serve with barbecued beans (see page 50).

Chicken and Pineapple Kebabs

Try using fresh pineapple if you can as tinned pineapple is often too sweet and doesn't really taste like the real thing.

1kg / 2lb chicken, cut into small pieces
1 small pineapple, peeled and cubed
20 shallots, peeled and blanched
2 red peppers, deseeded and cut into chunks
100g / 4oz button mushrooms

Marinade
1 tbsp of lemon juice
1 tbsp of walnut oil
1 tbsp white wine vinegar
2 cloves garlic, crushed
120ml / 4 fl oz soured cream
salt
freshly milled black pepper

Mix all the ingredients well with the marinade and chill for at least 3 hours. Then remove all the ingredients from the marinade and push them onto the skewers. Grill them on the barbecue for 15 minutes, turning and basting with the marinade every five minutes.

Serve the chicken and pineapple with a fresh tomato salad and a cold bottle of white wine.

SERVES 6

Curried Chicken Wings

Quick and easy to make, this is always the dish to go first at my barbecues. You can also use duck, rabbit or venison for this recipe.

24 chicken wings
3 cloves garlic, crushed
1 large onion, peeled and chopped
3 tbsp of mild curry paste
1 tsp crushed fennel seeds
150ml / 5 fl oz thick yoghurt
75g / 3oz melted butter
1 tbsp lemon juice
2 tbsp sweet sherry
1 tbsp Worcestershire sauce
salt
freshly milled black pepper

Trim the chicken wings and place them to one side. Place the other ingredients in a large bowl blending them thoroughly.

Add the chicken wings, ensuring they are completly covered. Let them stand for 3 hours, turning them every 15 minutes.

Place the wings onto the barbecue, grill and baste for at least 4-5 minutes on either side.

Heat the sauce on the barbecue for 6 minutes and serve with the chicken wings.

Scarborough
Seafood Kebabs

As you travel from Scarborough to Robin Hood's Bay and Whitby, reflect on a glorious tradition of Yorkshire seafood. This barbecue recipe deserves the freshest of ingredients, best found in the heart of Heartbeat country!

24 uncooked king prawns, shell removed
24 scallops, shell removed
24 oysters, shell removed
4 tbsp of oyster sauce
4 tbsp of fresh lemon juice
50g / 2oz clarified butter (see page 57)
1 tbsp sherry vinegar
3 tbsp sesame oil
freshly milled black pepper

Place all the ingredients into large bowl ar them to marinade for 24 hours.

Spear a king prawn, oyster and scallop or skewer.

Barbecue for 3-4 minutes, basting w marinade, seasoning again with freshly mill pepper before you serve them.

Place them onto a bed of shallots or onions and serve with chunks of garlic bread

SERVES 8

Salmon Steaks in Foil

Salmon is a versatile fish and you can add any combination of your favourite herbs, butter and oils to create your own personalized salmon steak in foil. My suggestion is below.

4 x 225g / 8oz salmon steaks,
buttered cooking foil
100g / 4oz unsalted butter
4 tbsp lemon juice
4 tbsp lime juice
freshly ground black pepper
4 tbsp freshly chopped parsley and chives

Place the salmon steaks onto individual pieces of cooking foil large enough to completely seal. Place 25g / 1oz of butter onto each salmon steak, dividing the rest of the ingredients between the four steaks.

Wrap the steaks in the foil, sealing them completely.

Place the fish in the fridge for 3 hours, and then bake the fish in the foil on the barbecue for 25 minutes, until the salmon is tender.

Carefully open the foil and remove the salmon from it onto individual plates, reserving the juices in the foil.

Remove the centre bone and outer skin around the salmon steak. Pour over the fish juices and serve with a sprig of fresh parsley, a little sour cream and freshly snipped chives.

SERVES 4

Prawns on Skewers

*Amazingly simple to prepare, yet always
a firm favourite.*

*900g / 2lb uncooked tiger prawns, shell removed
100g / 4oz sesame oil
3 cloves garlic, crushed
2 tbsp chopped parsley
150ml / 5 fl oz fresh lemon juice
salt
freshly milled black pepper*

Wash and dry the prawns. Toss the prawns in the other ingredients, ensuring that they are completely covered. Put all the ingredients in a flat baking tray,

Leave them to marinate for 3 hours, then put them onto skewers and barbecue them for 3 minutes either side, basting with the marinade.

Cheesy Baked Potatocs with Aidensfield Salad

There's nothing fancy about this recipe – but nothing is better than plain Yorkshire food.

*4 large baking potatoes
50g / 2oz butter
50g / 2oz grated Wensleydale cheese
4 tbsp soured cream
4 tsp snipped chives
salt
freshly milled black pepper
cooking foil*

Scrub the potatoes in warm water, dry and prick them all over with a fork.

Parboil them for 10 minutes in salted water. Dry them and cut a small wedge out of the centre.

Place on individual pieces of buttered cooking foil. Divide the butter, cheese, cream and chives equally between the potatoes, seasoning them and making sure there is enough room for the mix. Double wrap the potatos in the foil and cook on the top of the barbecue for 30 minutes.

Serve with Aidensfield salad (see following recipe).

SERVES 4

Aidensfield Salad

*Simple and nutritious, this is a mixture of
vegetables, fruit and herbs from the farms around
Aidensfield.*

175g / 6oz white cabbage, shredded
75g / 3oz celery, chopped
75g / 3oz carrot, grated
1 bunch of spring onions, cleaned, ends removed and snipped
2 leeks, cleaned and chopped
3 tomatoes, chopped
1 apple, cored, peeled and diced
4 tbsp mayonnaise (see recipe on page xxx)
1 tbsp freshly chopped basil
salt
freshly milled pepper
2 sprigs of fresh basil

Simply toss all the ingredients into a large salad
bowl, season with salt and freshly milled black
pepper and chill for 1 hour.
   Add a little chopped basil to garnish.

SERVES 6

Barbecued Beans

*The potato and corn on the cob are popular
vegetables at barbecues. However, a barby just isn't
complete without beans.*

25g / 1oz butter
1 large onion
100g / 4oz York ham, diced
1 tsp bought hickory smoked sauce
½ tsp crushed fennel seeds
1 tbsp American mustard
1 tbsp Worcestershire sauce
425g / 15oz beans in tomato sauce

Heat the butter in a large saucepan and fry the
onions and ham for 5 minute. Add all the rest of the
ingredients and simmer for 15 to 20 minutes on the
barbecue. Check the seasoning and add a little salt
and freshly milled black pepper.

SERVES 4

Apples in Foil

This makes a really nice accompaniment to pork and duck, or alternatively eat it as a dessert.

4 dessert apples, peeled and cored
50g / 2oz melted butter
1 tsp crushed cloves
1 tsp cinnamon
4 tbsp sultanas
4 large pieces of buttered cooking foil

Place each apple into the centre of a piece of buttered cooking foil

Put the butter, cloves, cinnamon and sultanas into a bowl and mix them together.

Pour a little of the mixture over each apple. Seal them very tightly and place them on the top of the barbecue for at least 20-25 minutes until they are cooked.

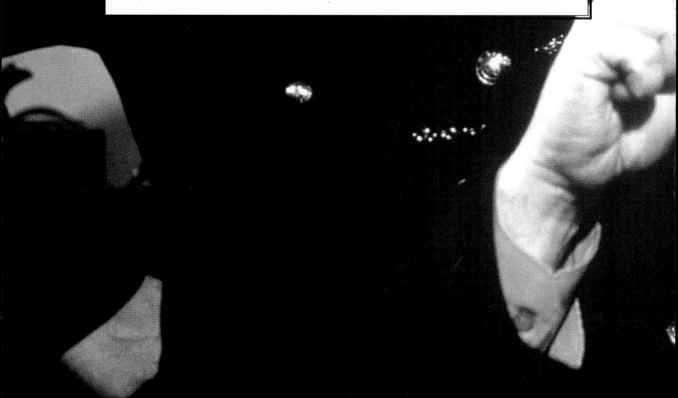

Chapter 5

Quick and Easy Light Lunch Recipes

Lunch is a very important part of Heartbeat life. It's a time when everyone can sit around the table and discuss the events of the morning while tucking into fresh warm bread and potted shrimps, Yorkshire sausages and cut-and-come-again cake.

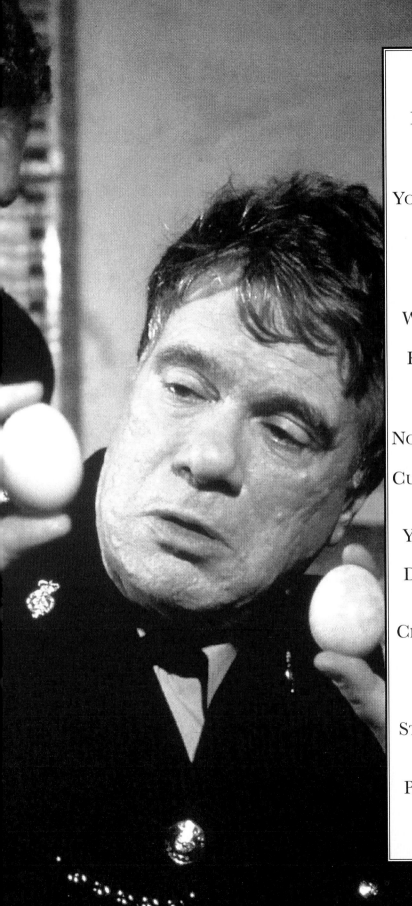

YORKSHIRE SAUSAGES

DEVILS ON HORSEBACK

POTTED CHEESE

YORKSHIRE POTTED CHEESE

SCOTCH WOODCOCK

A DELICIOUS SAVOURY

WHITBY POTTED SHRIMPS

KATE'S TOAD INTH' 'OLE

AIDENSFEILD FRITTERS

NORTH YORKSHIRE RAREBIT

CUT-AND-COME-AGAIN CAKE

LADY WHITLEY'S
YORKSHIRE BACON CAKES

DR RADCLIFFE'S PEARS IN
LEMON VINEGAR SAUCE

CRUNCHY CINNAMON APPLE
LAYERED YOGHURT

GOOSEBERRY FOOL

STRAWBERRY JAM FRITTERS
AND CREAM

POTTED SMOKED SALMON

OATCAKES

Yorkshire Sausages

These sausages were once the poor man's meatless meal, however, they are having a revival due to the popularity of vegetarian dishes. Served with a smooth creamy tomato sauce, these make an excellent light lunch.

175g / 6oz fresh breadcrumbs
100g / 4oz Cheddar cheese, grated
1 small leek, washed and finely chopped
pinch of mixed herbs and a pinch of mustard powder
salt
freshly milled black pepper
2 eggs, separated
4 tbsp fresh milk
crisp breadcrumbs for coating
25g / 1oz vegetable oil

Mix the breadcrumbs, cheese, leek, herbs and mustard, seasoning with salt and freshly ground black pepper in a large bowl.

Add 1 whole egg, the egg yolk of the second egg and a little milk to bind the mixture.

Divide the mixture into 6 or 8 pieces and shape into thick or thin sausages.

Whisk the remaining eggwhite until frothy and coat the sausages, first in the egg white and then in the breadcrumbs.

Heat the oil and fry the sausages for 6 minutes until golden brown. Serve with a little tomato sauce.

SERVES 4-6

Devils on Horseback

For a Devil on Horseback you stuff a prune with smoked bacon, but for an Angel on Horseback you stuff an oyster. I've outlined below a lavish alternative of the former.

8 prunes, destoned
8 hazelnuts, crushed
8 almonds, sliced
a little olive oil
a pinch of cayenne pepper
4 rashers of smoked streaky bacon, rindless
8 fried bread croutons
75g / 3oz Wensleydale cheese, grated

Stuff the prunes with the crushed hazelnuts and sliced almonds.

Sprinkle the prunes with a little olive oil and dust them with cayenne pepper.

Cut the smoked bacon in half and wrap a piece of bacon around each prune.

Put them onto a baking sheet and grill them until they are brown all over.

While they are grilling, sprinkle the grated cheese onto each crouton and place onto a warm serving plate. Place each prune onto the fried bread, sprinkle with a little more cayenne and serve.

SERVES 4

POTTED CHEESE

Potted cheese is rarely seen in recipe books and it would be a sad part of the cooking tradition if potted cheese recipes were to just die away. For this recipe I am going to show you how to make my Harlequin version of Richard Dolby's recipe from 1854. Richard Dolby was a well-respected cook at the Thatched House Tavern, St James Street in London. His potted cheese was served daily at Simpson's in the Strand, accompanied with West Riding Oatcakes.

Richard Dolby's Potted Cheese

Pound 3lb of North Wiltshire cheese with half pound of butter, a large glass of sherry and some ground mace. Mix well, pot it; and top with clarified butter.

SERVES 4

Yorkshire Potted Cheese (Author's Recipe)

125g / 4oz Wensleydale cheese
125g / 4oz Swaledale cheese
125g / 4oz Double Gloucester cheese
125g / 4oz Lancashire cheese
125g / 4oz Best Irish Butter
1 tbsp English mustard
150ml / 5 fl oz cream sherry
a large pinch of mace
a pinch of cayenne pepper
clarified butter (see page 57)
Oat Cakes (see page 63)
a bottle of good port

Crumble or grate the different cheeses, then place all the ingredients except the clarified butter into a blender and blend thoroughly, slowly adding the sherry.

Place into individual ramekins and pour over with clarified butter.

Allow the potted cheese to sit for at least 2 weeks. Serve with warm oat cakes and a very good vintage port.

Scotch Woodcock

Known also as Scots Woodcock, this is famous for its strong flavour of fresh anchovies and the unique custard sauce which was poured over during the 1840s when it was served as a main course. It is now eaten as a savoury or makes an ideal lunchtime snack.

4 slices of toasted bread, crust removed
25g / 1oz butter
8 anchovy fillets, pounded
4 egg yolks
300ml / 10 fl oz single cream
cayenne pepper
salt
freshly chopped parsley

Butter the hot toast and sandwich in pairs with the pounded anchovy filling.

Keep them warm. Blend the egg yolks with the cream, a pinch of cayenne and salt. Beat them together over some hot water. When the sauce is thick, pour it over the warm toast and sprinkle with chopped parsley.

SERVES 4

A Delicious Savoury

Anchovies, bread and cheese... it's simple!

4 slices of bread trimmed and fried in a little butter
16 anchovy fillets
225g / 8oz grated Cheshire cheese
chopped parsley
clarified butter(see page 57)

Place the anchovies onto the fried bread.

Cover with the cheese and chopped parsley. Pour over a little clarified butter. Grill until golden brown and serve.

SERVES 4

Whitby Potted Shrimps

I have several old recipes for potted shrimps as they have been popular in Yorkshire for over 250 years. Some recipes suggest you pound the shrimps beforehand while others tell you to season the shrimps with cloves and mace before pouring over 50g / 2oz melted butter.

450g / 1lb peeled shrimps
125g / 4oz melted butter
pinch of mace
pinch of nutmeg
pinch of crushed cloves
a little salt
freshly ground black pepper
clarified butter
brown bread and butter
thin slices of lemon
sprigs of fresh parsley

Place all the ingredients into a small saucepan and bring them gradually to a warm heat, making sure that the contents do not boil.

Place into small ramekins, covering them with clarified butter and chill in the refrigerator for at least 2 hours before serving.

Serve with a sprig of fresh parsley, slices of fresh lemon, brown bread and butter.

SERVES 4-6

Authors tip: Clarified Butter.

Use 225g / 8oz of butter, which will give you 175g / 6oz of clarified butter.

Place the butter into a small saucepan and heat very gently, skimming off the foam as the butter heats.

The sediment sinks to the bottom of the pan as the butter heats. When completely melted, remove the pan from the heat and leave it to stand for a least 4 minutes. Strain the butter through a cheesecloth or fine cotton into a bowl.

Allow the butter to cool a little before pouring it over the surface of the potted shrimps.

Kate's Toad Inth' 'ole

A real Yorkshire favourite made into small individual bite-size cakes which are delicious. A great deal of fun can be had by adding anything you wish into toad in the hole. In the past I have used snails, alligator tails, frogs' legs, and every type of fowl and game. Warne's Model Cookery, *published in 1868, gives the following recipe:*

❝TOAD IN A HOLE

A chicken; some veal stuffing; three eggs; one pint of milk; some flour. Draw, bone, and truss a chicken, fill it with a veal stuffing. Make a batter with a pint of milk, three eggs, and sufficient flour to make it thick; pour it into a buttered dish. Place the fowl in the centre of the batter, and bake it in the oven. Serve in the same dish. ❞

For my recipe I am going to use Cumberland sausage, but you can use, pork, beef or even vegetarian sausage.

450g / 1lb Cumberland sausage
30ml / 2 tbsp beef dripping
100g / 4oz plain flour
a pinch of salt
1 fresh large egg
200ml / 7 fl oz fresh milk
100ml / 3 fl oz water

Pre-heat the oven to gas mark 7, 220°C / 425°F.

Mix the flour and a pinch of salt into a large bowl, make a well in the centre and add the egg.

Add half the milk and, using a wooden spoon, work it into the flour slowly. Beat the mixture until it is smooth, then add the remaining milk and water, and beat until this is smooth. Let the mixture stand for at least 1 hour.

Put the dripping into the individual pattie tins or one large baking tin.

Cut up the sausage so that you get a generous piece in each individual tray.

Place into the oven for 5 minutes until the tray is very hot, remove and pour in the batter, leaving room at the top for the mixture to expand.

Return to the oven to cook for 35 minutes, until risen and golden brown. Do not open the oven door at all for at least 30 minutes.

Serve while they are hot with a good beef gravy.(see page 138)

SERVES 4-6

Aidensfield Fritters

Aidensfield fritters are made in the same way as fishcakes. Every county has its own style of fritter, and I am sure you have a favourite version of your own. Like the Toad inth' 'ole, it's a filling meal that doesn't cost a great deal of money and you can use any leftover bits of meat, fish or poultry that you have lying around in your fridge.

450g / 1lb buttered mashed potato
100g / 4oz cheddar, grated
100g / 4oz fresh brown breadcrumbs
225g / 8oz York ham, finely chopped
1 tbsp mixed herbs
salt
freshly milled black pepper
2 eggs
milk
75g / 3oz cooking oil

Blend the ham, potatoes, cheese, herbs and 1 egg in a large bowl, seasoning well with salt and freshly ground black pepper.

Shape the mixture into small balls or flat pancakes. Beat the second egg with a little milk.

Place the breadcrumbs on a plate. Pass the balls through the egg mixture and roll them into the breadcrumbs until they are coated.

Heat the cooking oil in a large frying pan and cook the fritters until they are golden brown.

SERVES 4-6

North Yorkshire Rarebit

No cheese other than Wensleydale will do!

225g / 8oz Wensleydale
15ml / 1 tbsp butter
15ml / 1 tbsp Worcestershire sauce
5ml / 1 tsp dry English mustard
10ml / 2 tsp plain flour
60ml / 4 tbsp Tetley's bitter
salt
freshly milled black pepper
4 slices of bread toasted on both sides
sprig of fresh parsley

Place the cheese, butter, Worcestershire sauce, mustard, beer and seasoning into a saucepan mixing all the ingredients together. Gently bring the mixture to the boil and remove from the heat.

Whisk it until it becomes quite creamy in texture and allow it to cool.

Toast the bread and spread the rarebit over the toast and place under a hot grill until bubbling and golden brown.

Sprinkle with a little parsley and serve.

SERVES 4

Author's tip: Add 125g / 4oz Mozzarella with 150ml / 5 fl oz double cream to the above ingredients for an excellent summer fondue. Serve with summer fruits and bread sticks.

Cut-and-Come-Again Cake

I'm sure people are interested to hear the story of how this fruitcake got its name. The ladies of the Moors would meet for afternoon tea and bring with them the leftovers from their morning's baking – a few ounces of sultanas or currants, or maybe some flour or butter. These leftovers would then be given to the woman whose turn it was to host the tea for the following week, and with her collection of ingredients she would bake a Cut-and-Come-Again cake.

175g / 6oz butter
275g / 10 fl oz self-raising flour
175g / 6oz brown sugar
100g / 4oz currants
30ml / 2 tbsp dark rum
100g / 4oz sultanas
100g / 4oz raisins
50g / 2oz mixed chopped peel
25g / 1oz ginger, freshly grated
pinch of cinnamon
4 fresh eggs, well beaten

Pre-heat the oven to Gas mark 4, 180°C / 350°F.

Rub the flour and butter together to form very fine crumbs. Blend in all the other ingredients.

Lightly grease a 20-cm (8 inch) cake tin.

Bake in the oven for an hour and a half. Cool in the tin, then remove and serve with cheese.

SERVES 6-8

Lady Whitley's Yorkshire Bacon Cakes

Grand though she is, Lady Whitley knows how to cook proper Yorkshire food. Her splendid bacon cakes are a favourite with her estate workers at any time of the year.

75g / 3oz cooked crisp bacon, cut into small pieces
225g / 8oz self-raising flour (sifted with a pinch of salt)
25g / 1oz softened butter
100g / 4oz Swaledale cheese, grated
150ml / ¼ pint fresh milk
1 tbsp tomato puree
1 egg, whisked

Pre-heat the oven to gas mark 6, 200°C / 400°F.

Add the sifted flour into a bowl and gently rub the softened butter with it. Add the bacon and 50g / 2oz of the cheese. Mix the milk and tomato puree together and add this to the dry ingredients to make a soft dough.

Place the mixture onto a floured board and roll out a 20cm / 8 inch circle. Brush with the egg and cut into 8 even wedges.

Place onto a hot greased baking tray, sprinkle with the remaining Swaledale cheese and bake for 25 minutes.

SERVES 4-6

Dr Radcliffe's Pears in Lemon Vinegar Sauce

I always use Williams or Comice pears for this recipe.

4 Ripe Pears

Dressing
4 tbsp lemon and blackpepper vinegar
1 tsp warm honey
4 tbsp virgin olive oil
1 tsp prepared English mustard
juice of 1 lemon and zest
1 small clove garlic, crushed
salt

Mix the above ingredients in a bowl.

Peel the pears and cutting them in half, carefully remove the core with a spoon.

Turn the pears very carefully into the vinegar sauce and leave them to chill for at least 3 hours.

In the meantime, wash and clean the following leaves:

100g / 4oz assorted salad leaves
225g / 8oz cooked asparagus spears, chopped
75g / 3oz black and green seedless grapes
8 sprigs of fennel for garnish

Wash and clean the leaves then toss them with the asparagus and grapes.

Place the pears onto the serving dish flat side down and carefully slice them into a fan shape. Pour over a little of the vinegar sauce and then pour the remaining sauce onto the salad. Toss the salad and place a small selection of leaves at the side of each pear.

Garnish each pear with a sprig of fennel. Serve with brown bread and butter.

SERVES 4

Crunchy Cinnamon Apple Layered with Yoghurt

An ideal finish to a light lunch. Yorkshire Bramleys are the obvious selection here.

450g / 1lb pureed apples
50g/ 2oz digestive biscuits, crushed
25g / 1oz soft brown sugar
1 tsp cinnamon
150ml / ¼ pint plain or friut yoghurt
sprig of fresh mint

Put the crushed digestive biscuits, cinnamon and brown sugar into a bowl and blend.

Pour a layer of yoghurt into four large stem wine glasses. Follow this with a layer of apple puree, then yoghurt again.

Repeat the process and top with a tablespoon of the cinnamon crunch you have in the bowl, and a sprig of fresh mint.

To make the recipe even better, add fresh fruits to the yoghurt and sweeten the apple puree with a little clear honey.

SERVES 4-6

Gooseberry Fool

Yorkshire's Egton Bridge Old Gooseberry Society was formed in 1800 and is renowned for the world's biggest gooseberries. For a real taste of old England, try this fool recipe which dates back to Tudor times. If you don't like gooseberries, use another type of non-citrus fruit like rhubarb or strawberries.

575g / 1¼lb gooseberries, washed, topped and tailed
225g / 8oz caster sugar
3 eggs
450ml / 15 fl oz milk
300ml / 10 fl oz double cream

Cook the gooseberries with 175g / 6oz of the sugar in a large pan for 15 minutes until they are very soft.

Put the milk on to boil then allow it to cool slightly.

Beat the eggs and remaining sugar in a large basin. Add the milk, whisking thoroughly.

Stand the basin in a pan of boiling water, keeping the pan of water under boiling point until the contents begin to thicken.

Stir the custard all the time for about 4 minutes then take the basin from the hot water and allow it to cool.

The gooseberries should now be cooked, so rub them through a fine sieve. Allow the puree to become cold.

Whip the double cream until it stands in stiff peaks, add the custard and gooseberry puree and mix until they are all blended.

Serve in individual glasses topped with whipped cream and slices of fresh gooseberry.

SERVES 4

Strawberry Jam Fritters and Cream

A dessert which has numerous permutations. You can stuff the bread and butter filling with numerous fruits and it can be served with a rich custard sauce, clotted cream, fromage frais or home-made ice cream.

8 slices of thickly buttered bread, spread with a generous amount of home-made strawberry jam.
flour
sweet batter (see recipe below)
300ml / 10 fl oz corn oil
300ml / 10 fl oz double cream

Sweet Batter Recipe
100g / 4oz plain flour
25g / 1oz icing sugar
1 egg
150ml / 5 fl oz fresh milk

Sift the flour and icing sugar into a bowl.

Make a well into the centre of the mixture and add the egg.

Add half the milk and using a whisk, gradually work it into the flour.

Slowly add the remaining milk to make a smooth batter.

Remove the crusts from the bread and quarter the slices.

Heat the oil in a shallow pan until it is smoking.

Flour the sandwich quarters and dip them into the batter.

Deep fry them until golden brown.

Dust with a little icing sugar and serve with whipped double cream.

SERVES 4-6

Potted Smoked Salmon

Smoked salmon is expensive but you can buy the cheaper ends of smoked salmon from your fishmonger or the supermarket. Salmon ends are the trimmings from smoked salmon fillets.

350g / 12oz smoked salmon ends
a pinch of grated nutmeg
a pinch of mace
100g / 4oz butter, softened
salt
freshly ground black pepper
2 tbsp port
2 tbsp double cream
1 lemon, thinly sliced
sprigs of parsley

Place the chopped smoked salmon ends into a large bowl with all the ingredients, except the lemon and parsley. Pound until the mixture is very smooth.

Place into individual earthenware pots. Cover with buttered greaseproof paper and place in the refrigerator for 4 hours. Remove the paper and dress with slices of fresh lemon and parsley.

Serve with warm toast and butter.

SERVES 4-6

Oatcakes

A centuries-old traditional Yorkshire recipe.

225g / 8oz fine oatmeal
100g / 4oz wholemeal flour
1 tsp salt
25g / 1oz fresh yeast, dissolved in 600ml/ 20 fl oz tepid milk and water (use a half and half measure)

Sift the oatmeal, flour and salt into a clean mixing bowl and add the tepid liquid slowly to make a smooth batter. Leave the mixture to stand in a warm place for 45 minutes.

Mix well with floured hands and turn the mixture onto a surface and shape the mixture into small flat cakes.

Grease a heavy based frying pan and cook on both sides in the corn oil for 3 minutes on a medium heat.

Traditionally, the oatcakes were then hung on the clothes line until they dried. But I advise you to allow them to dry on a baking sheet for about 15 minutes. Butter them and serve them with cheese.

SERVES 4-6

Chapter 6

Autumn
Recipes

Autumn brings some of the finest fish to the waters of the Yorkshire coast. Nick buys his sea bream, brill and crabs for Kate from Whitby, which is also well known for its oysters, sole, grey mullet and kippers. Scarborough is just a stone's throw from Heartbeat country and I am sure these recipes will be well received by all of Aidensfield's inhabitants.

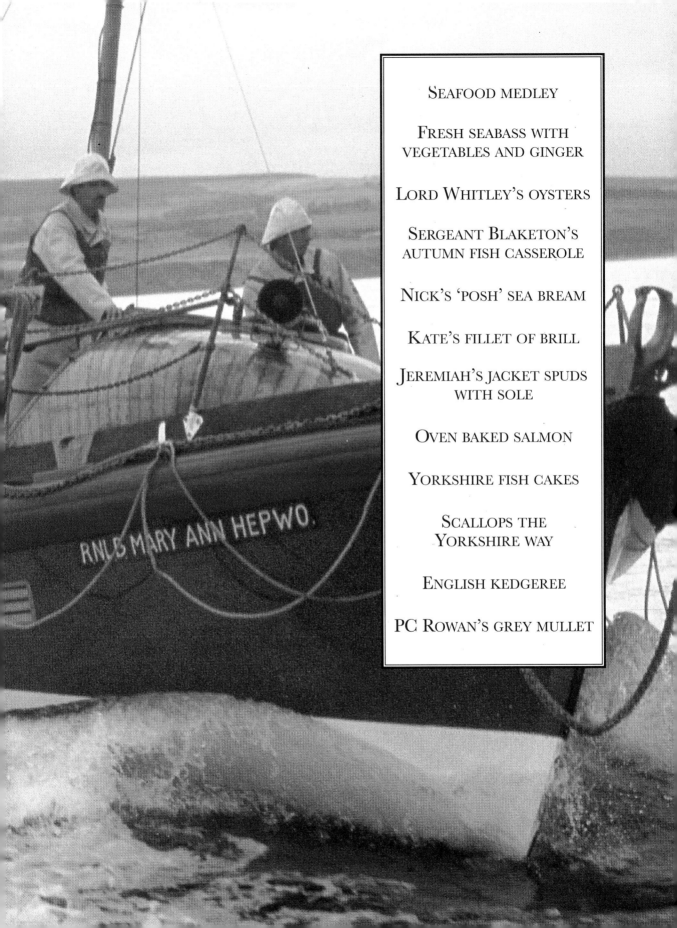

SEAFOOD MEDLEY

FRESH SEABASS WITH
VEGETABLES AND GINGER

LORD WHITLEY'S OYSTERS

SERGEANT BLAKETON'S
AUTUMN FISH CASSEROLE

NICK'S 'POSH' SEA BREAM

KATE'S FILLET OF BRILL

JEREMIAH'S JACKET SPUDS
WITH SOLE

OVEN BAKED SALMON

YORKSHIRE FISH CAKES

SCALLOPS THE
YORKSHIRE WAY

ENGLISH KEDGEREE

PC ROWAN'S GREY MULLET

Seafood Medley on a Bed of Rose Petal Cream Sauce

You can use all types of seafood in this recipe. Nick always tries to use red seabream, and when he is choosing his fish he checks the gills and eyes for freshness. The eyes should be bright and bulbous. If they are flat, dull or sunken, then the fish should be rejected. The gills should be moist and red and the body firm to the touch, not slimy. And, remember, a fresh, healthy fish should not smell 'fishy' at all!

12 scallops, off the shell
12 tiger prawns
12 crevettes
450g / 1lb bream
125g / 4oz freshwater prawns
50g / 2oz butter
juice and zest of 1 lemon

For the Sauce
150ml / ¼ pint rose petal vinegar
150ml / ¼ pint white wine
1rbs lemon juice
8 pink peppercorns
pinch saffron
salt
freshly milled black pepper
150ml / ¼ pint double cream or fromage frais

Vegetable Stock
1 carrot, diced
1 onion, diced
1 stick of celery, sliced
1 leek, chopped
bouquet garni
1 clove of garlic

Boil the vegetables in 1 litre of water and the bouquet garni. Simmer for 1 hour to make the vegetable stock, strain and place to one side.

Fillet the seabream, slice and place to one side.

Place the crevettes onto their sides and cut down the spine with a sharp knife.

Melt the butter in a large saucepan and sauté the seafood and fish for about 2 to 3 minutes. Season with ground black pepper. Add the lemon juice and zest.

Add a pinch of saffron powder or a few saffron strands to the juice and butter in the pan.

Remove the pan from the heat and place the seafood onto a warm plate. Place into the oven to keep warm.

Return the pan and heat up the juice. Add the vegetable stock and bring to the boil until the liquid is reduced by one third.

Add the rose petal vinegar and boil for 4 minutes.

Add the peppercorns, lemon juice and white wine and let it reduce for a further 6 minutes.

Add the cream and simmer for 2 minutes.

Remove the fish from the oven and lightly coat the fish with the sauce.

Should you be serving this as a main course, mash the vegetables left from the stock with some potatoes and make them into little patty shapes. Coat with egg and breadcrumbs, and shallow fry them in a little melted butter or cooking oil.

SERVES 8-10

Fresh Seabass with Vegetables and Ginger

Around Whitby and Scarborough the salty smell of the North Sea brings fresh fish to mind and the appetite gets bigger.

Stuffing

50g / 2oz each of the following carrot, leek and celeriac, julienned
50g / 2oz mange tout
2g / ½oz fresh ginger, cut into fine strips
150ml / ¼ pint white wine
150ml / ¼ pint crème fraiche or double cream
salt
freshly milled black pepper

The Seabass

8 x 100g / 4oz sized seabass medallions.

The Sauce

25g / 1oz butter
4 shallots, peeled and chopped
10 cardamon pods
2 star anise
1 tbsp crushed coriander seeds
trimmings from the ginger
black pepper
300ml / ½ pint of white wine
300ml / ½ pint fish stock
seasoning
300ml / ½ pint double cream or fromage frais
juice of 1 lemon

Blanch the ginger for five minutes in boiling water. Cook the carrot, leek, celeriac and mange tout in the white wine.

When reduced and nearly cooked, add the ginger and cream. Reduce again until the stuffing is thick. Season and cool.

With a sharp knife, cut a pocket into the medallion and stuff with the julienne of vegetables.

Cook the shallots in the butter for 4 minutes, add the spices and cook for a further 3 minutes.

Add the wine and fish stock, reduce by half, add the cream, reduce again by half.

Season well with salt and freshly milled black pepper. Add the lemon juice.

Pour the sauce over the medallions and garnish with fresh slices of lemon and shredded leek and carrot.

This sauce can also be used for the scallops recipe on page 74.

SERVES 4-6

Lord Whitley's Oyster's

What more can one say: they're damned good!

12 oysters
50g / 2oz best butter
50g / 2oz plain flour
300ml / 10 fl oz dry white wine
2 shallots, finely chopped
1 tbsp finely chopped parsley
1 tsp anchovy essence
salt
freshly milled black pepper
175g / 6oz white crabmeat
75g / 3oz Wensleydale cheese
75g / 3oz Stilton cheese
125g / 4oz smoked salmon
175g / 6oz fresh breadcrumbs
1 small jar of caviar
1 thinly sliced lemon

Poach the oysters in their own juice for 4 minutes.

Strain the juice into another saucepan. Melt the butter in a saucepan and add the flour. Cook for 2 minutes, blending all the time.

Add the white wine and shallots, bring to the boil and add the oyster juice.

Let the mixture reduce by one third.

Add the parsley, anchovy essence and season well. Cook for a further 15 minutes. Remove the pan from the heat and carefully blend in the oysters and crabmeat.

Spoon the mixture into individual 1/2 pint ramekins or gratin dishes and sprinkle with both cheeses. Top with a little smoked salmon and breadcrumbs.

Bake in the oven for 12 minutes.

Top with a little Caviar and a piece of lemon before serving with garlic bread.

SERVES 2

Sergeant Blaketon's Autumn Fish Casserole

Yorkshire is one of the most picturesque places in Europe and I have friends from all over the world who always enjoy visiting this part of England – not just for their favourite beer, but for the day trips to Ilkley, Doncaster, and my favourite, the town of Shipley, where this fish casserole comes from. I've poached this recipe from Sergeant Blaketon as it's a favourite of his too.

450g / 1lb brill fillets, skinned and chopped
450g / 1lb hake fillets, skinned and chopped
75g / 3oz plain flour
salt
freshly milled black pepper
75g / 3oz butter
4 shallots, skinned and finely chopped
1 carrot, peeled and diced
1 leek, washed, and finely chopped
300ml / ½ pint of fish stock
300ml / ½ pint of medium dry white wine
2 tsp anchovy essence
1 tbsp tarragon vinegar
chopped fresh parsley

Coat the fish in 25g / 1oz of seasoned flour. Melt the butter in a flameproof casserole and add the fish, onion, carrot and leeks. Cook gently for 10 minutes.

Sprinkle with the remaining flour, stirring for 2 minutes.

Slowly add the fish stock, wine, anchovy essence and tarragon vinegar.

Bring to the boil and simmer for 35 minutes on a low heat or bake in the oven for 30 minutes at gas mark 4, 180°C / 350°F.

Sprinkle with freshly chopped parsley and serve with warm crusty brown bread and a green salad.

SERVES 4-6

Nick's 'Posh' Seabream

'Going on the motorbike to Whitby on Thursday nights is a trip I don't really enjoy but I can pick up my fresh fish and my favourite wines for just 15 shillings and sixpence.'

4 x 175g / 6oz seabream
25g / 1oz butter
2 tbsp olive oil
1 cucumber
150ml / ¼ pint fish stock
150ml / ¼ pint red wine
1 tbsp lemon juice
3 tbsp double cream
1 tsp tomato puree
25g / 1oz butter and plain flour, mixed
4 shallots, finely chopped
1 tsp freshly chopped parsley

In a deep frying pan melt the butter and cook the shallots for 1 minute. Add the wine and lemon juice. Reduce by half.

Add the tomato puree and fish stock cook until the mixture has reduced.

Season to taste. Add the butter and flour into the sauce. While the sauce is simmering grill the fish by placing it on buttered foil and grilling lightly for a few minutes.

Peel the cucumber into long strips, then toss them in a little olive oil.

Pour the sauce into the centre of the plate, Carefully place the bream at the side and garnish with parsley. Place a spoonful of cream at the side and top it with the cucumber strips.

SERVES 4-6

Kate's Fillet of Brill

*Brill and spinach are high in vitamins and iron.
The combination of these two ingredients will keep
your skin in perfect condition.*

*4 x 175g / 6oz brill fillets, bones and skin removed
225g / 8oz spinach, cooked
125g / 4oz Vegetables cut into fine strips
2 tbsp olive oil
100ml / 3½ fl oz dry white wine
2 shallots, chopped
1 tbsp lemon juice
12 pink peppercorns
50ml / 2oz fish stock
25g / 1oz plain flour
25ml / 1 fl oz double cream
freshly chopped parsley
salt
freshly milled black peppercorns
1 tbsp chopped chives*

Season the fillets of brill with a little salt and freshly milled pepper.

Put the wine, fish stock, parsley, shallots, peppercorns and lemon juice into a deep saute pan.

Bring the liquid to the boil and simmer for 5 minutes.

Place the brill fillets into the stock and slowly simmer for 3 minutes.

Re-heat the spinach and place into the centre of each plate.

Carefully remove the brill from the pan and leave the stock cooking until it has reduced by at least a third.

Place the brill fillets on the top of the spinach and keep warm.

Put the olive oil into a frying pan and heat until it is very hot.

Quickly blanch the vegetables in the hot oil, drain and place on the top of the brill.

Add the flour and the cream to the stock, cook for 1 minute or until it thickens and then pour the sauce around the brill. Garnish with lemon slices and chopped chives.

Jeremiah's Jacket Spuds with Sole

The Victorians called these jacket potatoes 'Soles in their Coffins' and even today they are ideal for feasting on during the dark autumn nights.

6 large baked potatoes
salt
freshly milled black pepper
12 small fillets of sole
4 shallots, finely chopped
150ml / 5 fl oz red wine
75g / 3oz butter
100g / 4oz button mushrooms, sliced
50g / 2oz seasoned plain flour, sifted
300ml / ½ pint of warm milk
2 tbsp double cream
175g / 6oz fresh water prawns
1 sprig of fresh fennel

Pre-heat the oven to gas mark 6, 200°C / 400°F

Coat each fillet with a little wine, season them well and roll them up with the skinned side inwards, holding them together with a small wooden skewer.

Poach them in the red wine for about 4 minutes. Carefully remove the fish from the pan, reserving the juice.

In another saucepan add 50g / 1oz butter and cook the mushroom and shallots for 2 minutes. Add the seasoned flour. Slowly add the red wine stock and half the milk.

Simmer for 4 minutes , re-adjusting the seasoning. Remove the sauce from the heat. Blend in the double cream

Using a tablespoon, carefully scoop out the centres of the jacket potatoes and mash them.

Place the potato shells on a greased baking sheet . Remove the skewers from the fillets of sole. Put two sole fillets into each potato with some prawns and a little red wine sauce, pipe on the mashed potato and bake them for 8 minutes and finish them off under a hot grill for 2 minutes to brown.

Serve them with the red wine sauce, garnished with prawns and a sprig of fresh fennel.

Oven Baked Salmon

*The best of British food combined with a serving of
herb creamed potato and baked Bramley apples.*

4 x 225g / 8oz Salmon fillets
50g / 2oz melted butter
salt
freshly milled black pepper
1 tsp crushed fennel seeds
4 tbsp fresh breadcrumbs
1 tbsp poppy seeds
4 small Bramley apples, cored and filled with a little grated
nutmeg and a sprig of mint and fennel
450g / 1lb potato blended with 1 tsp freshly ground mint and
fennel.
4 tbsp melted butter

Pre-heat the oven gas mark 6, 200°C / 400°F.

Grease a baking tray with the butter, place the
salmon fillets on the baking tray, with the rest of the
butter glazed on top of the salmon.

Put all the dry ingredients into a bowl and mix
them together.

Sprinkle onto the salmon fillets.

Place the apples on the same tray and bake in the
oven for 20 minutes.

Remove the salmon fillets onto a serving dish and
return the apples to the oven for a further 15
minutes until they are cooked.

Put the warmed creamed potato into a piping bag
and pipe around the salmon fillets, saving a little of
the creamed potato as a bed for the baked apples.
Keep the salmon warm.

When the apples are cooked, place them onto the
corner of each piece of salmon. Pour a tablespoon
of the melted butter onto the salmon, adding any of
the juice from the baking tray.

SERVES 4

Yorkshire Fish Cakes

*Fish cakes should look like proper fish cakes and not
like the tiny bite-size morsels that you see on
television, deep frozen or in a packet. There's
nothing artificial in my recipe here.*

50g / 2oz butter
450g / 1lb poached haddock or cod fillet
450g / 1lb mashed potato
100g / 4oz Wensleydale cheese, grated
1 large egg, blended with 1 tbsp of cream
salt
freshly milled black pepper
1 tbsp Worcestershire sauce
1 tbsp anchovy essence
25g / 1oz sifted flour
1 egg whisked with a little milk
175g / 6oz fine white breadcrumbs
50g / 2oz beef dripping
1 sprig of fresh sage
1 lemon cut into wedges
1 bottle of thick tomato sauce

Melt the butter in a saucepan over a low heat and
add the flaked fish. Beat in the potato, cheese and
egg mixture. Season the fish cake mixture with salt
and freshly milled black pepper. Add the
Worcestershire sauce and anchovy essence.

Spread the mixture onto a floured surface and
form the mixture into 4-6 large fish cakes.

Dip the cakes into the eggwash and then into the
breadcrumbs, repeat this process twice.

Fry the fish cakes in the hot dripping until golden
brown, about 4 minutes on either side. Serve with a
fresh sage leaf, a lemon wedge and some thick
tomato sauce.

SERVES 4

Scallops the Yorkshire Way

I have eaten scallops all over the world, but nowhere are they cooked to perfection as in Yorkshire where the best cooks are born and bred: Elizabeth Raffald, Michael Smith and our very own Marco Pierre White to name but a few. I feel that scallops should not be removed from their shells during the cooking process and most Yorkshire folk will agree with me.

24 scallops and corals
4 tbsp mushroom soy
4 tbsp snipped chives
1 tbsp chopped oregano
1 tbsp of Worcesterhire sauce
3 tbsp fresh lemon juice
25g / 1oz melted butter
2 cloves garlic, crushed
4 tbsp Yorkshire relish (see recipe 130)
4 tbsp of white wine

Garnish
fresh chives
lemon wedges

Pre-heat the oven gas mark 6, 200°C / 400°F.

Open the scallops carefully and pour any juices from them into a large bowl. Clean and wash any excess sand or dirt from the inside and outside of the shell, taking care not to disturb the scallop and not to break the coral.

Add the rest of the ingredients to the bowl and mix them thoroughly.

Place the scallops onto a baking tray and add a generous tablespoon of the sauce onto each scallop.

Bake in the oven for 8 minutes and serve with fresh chives and lemon wedges, brown bread and butter.

SERVES 6

English Kedgeree

Originally a spicy Indian recipe, Kitchri contained onions and lentils. It was brought back to England in the eighteenth century by the nabobs of the East India Company.

450g / 1lb cooked haddock, bones and skin removed
175g / 6oz long-grain rice, cooked
salt
freshly ground black pepper
saffron powder
3 hard boiled eggs, shelled
2 tbsp double cream
50g / 2oz butter
freshly chopped parsley
coriander leaves

Flake the cooked haddock, making sure that all the bones and skin are removed.

Melt the butter in a saucepan, add the fish and a pinch of saffron. Chop the eggs and add them with the rice to the saucepan.

Gently heat all the ingredients together. Slowly add the cream, stirring thoroughly, and season with salt and freshly ground black pepper. Serve hot with a sprinkling of freshly chopped parsley or coriander leaves.

SERVES 6

PC Rowan's Grey Mullet

This dish is now served in numerous Chinese and Japanese restaurants around Great Britain, yet it is originally a West Yorkshire recipe from the eighteenth century. I suspect that PC Rowan brought this with him from London's Chinatown area where he worked his old beat.

4 X 275g / 10oz Grey mullet, gutted and cleaned
300ml / 10 fl oz dry white wine
4 shallots, finely chopped
1 clove of garlic, crushed
a small bunch of fresh herbs
finely grated rind and juice of 1 lemon
a pinch of fresh nutmeg
3 anchovy fillets, roughly chopped
salt
freshly ground black pepper
2 tbsp double cream mixed with 5ml / 1 tsp cornflour

Garnish
sprig of fresh mint
slices of lemon and lemon zest

Pre-heat the oven to gas mark 4, 180°C / 350°F.

Put all the ingredients except those for the garnish, into a large casserole, cover and bake in the oven for 35 minutes.

Remove the mullet very carefully onto a warm serving dish and keep warm in the oven.

Bring the fish stock to the boil and reduce by half, simmering for 25 minutes. Thicken with a little double cream mixed with cornflour.

Pour the sauce over the mullet and garnish with a sprig of fresh mint and slices of lemon and zest.

SERVES 4

Chapter 7

Pie Society Country

Every area of Yorkshire has its very own pie recipe so this book would be incomplete without this section. Traditional steak and kidney, apple and pork, my three layer cheese pie, stand pie, chicken and mushroom pie and the famous Aidensfield tattie pie are just a few of the mouthwatering recipes covered here. George Ward, the landlord of The Aidensfield Arms, and his beautiful niece Gina have made nearly all of these pies for their regular visitors to the pub.

Traditional steak and kidney pie

Claude Jeremiah's apple and pork pie

Three layer cheese pie

Veal, ham and egg pie

Chicken and ham pie

Stand pie

Grouse pie

Venison pasty

Aidensfield tattie pie

Gina's Apple and blackberry pie

Fish pie

Yorkshire mint pasties

Game pie

Short crust pastry

Puff pastry

Traditional Steak and Kidney Pie

*This most popular pie is everyone's favourite —
not only in Heartbeat country but around
Great Britain too. Do not cheat with cheaper cuts
of meat; use the best rump steak and ox kidneys
· to acheive the perfect pie.*

575g / 1¼lb rump steak
175g / 6oz ox kidneys
1 large onion
300ml / ½ pint beef stock
25g / 1oz seasoned flour
225g / 8oz shortcrust pastry (page 91)
25g / 1oz butter
salt
freshly milled black pepper

Trim the steak and cut into 2.5cm / 1 inch cubes.

Remove the fat, skin and core from the kidney and dice.

Toss the steak and kidney into the seasoned flour.

Melt the butter into a large frying pan and quickly seal the meat all over, adding the chopped onion. Cook for 4 minutes.

Add the beef stock, season and simmer for a further 25 minutes.

While the beef is simmering, line a large, well-greased pudding basin with the shortcrust pastry, leaving enough pastry to make a lid.

Put the steak, kidney and stock into the basin and top with the lid, damping the edges with water to make it stick.

Cover the basin with buttered tin foil or greaseproof paper.

Stand the basin in a large saucepan with enough water to half cover the basin.

Finally Bring the water to the boil and steam for 2 hours, making sure you top the water, so the pan will not dry.

Serve with fresh carrots, mashed and roast potatoes.

SERVES 6

Claude Jeremiah's Apple and Pork Pie

Apple and pork pie, served cold with pickles and chunks of cheese, makes up your typical Yorkshire ploughman's lunch. Greengrass, however, might eat this at night when up to no good!

900g / 2lb roughly minced pork
50g / 2oz onion, chopped
150ml / ¼ pint dry white wine
2 tbsp brandy
½ tsp dried sage
1 tbsp Dijon mustard
1 Bramley apple, peeled and grated coarsely
salt
freshly ground black pepper

Stuffing
175g / 6oz packet stuffing (sage and onion)
50g / 2oz onion, minced
50g/ 2oz bramley apples
150ml / 5 fl oz beef stock
225g/8oz black pudding, mashed with skin removed
aspic
hot water pastry (see page 82)
egg glaze
aspic jelly made with a little wine and pork stock

Pre heat the oven to gas mark 6, 200°C / 400°F

Mix the minced pork with the onion, wine, brandy, sage, Dijon mustard and apple. Season this with a generous pinch of salt and some fresh ground black pepper.

Line the bottom of each pie mould with hot water pastry.

Fill the lined tin with the meat mixture and then the stuffing mixture alternating until you have three layers of pork and two of stuffing .

Roll out the remaining pastry to make a lid to fit the pie.

Make a hole in the centre of the pie lid.

Decorate with pastry leaves, egg glaze and bake for 35 minutes. Reduce the oven to gas mark 4, 180°C / 350°F and continue to bake for a further 1 hour.

Remove the pie from the oven and allow it to cool.

Pour in some aspic jelly, made up with a little wine and pork stock.

When the aspic has set, wrap the pie in clingfilm and allow to mature for two days.

SERVES 6

Three Layer Cheese Pie

This pie is my own contribution to Heartbeat country cooking, and it really is something else!
Use three different coloured cheeses for contrast. When layered with spinach, fruit and onions you
get a lovely marbled effect which you can see when you slice into the pie. Use red Leicester, mature
yellow Cheddar and white Wensleydale cheeses. Wensleydale, I think, is the most underr-rated
of all British cheeses – it's certainly my favourite.

350g / 12oz shortcrust pastry (page 91)
50g / 2oz butter
450g / 1lb onions, chopped
350g / 12oz spinach leaf, trimmed, blanched and chopped
175g / 6oz each of the following grated cheeses:
red Leicestershire, mature yellow Cheddar and Wensleydale
4 tbsp apple puree
4 tbsp gooseberry puree
4 tbsp cranberry sauce
1 tsp freshly grated nutmeg
salt
freshly milled black pepper
3 tsp Worcestershire sauce
1 egg mixed with 1 tbsp milk

Pre-heat the oven to gas mark 5, 190°C / 375°F.

Roll out the pastry and use two-thirds of it to line a deep 25cm / 10 inch ring pie tin or loose-based cake tin, greased with a little butter

Fry the onion in a little butter for 3 minutes. Add the spinach and cook for 2 minutes, seasoning well with freshly milled black pepper and a little salt.

Layer the spinach and onion at the base of the pie, then top with the red Leicester and apple puree.

Then add another layer of spinach and onion, topping with the Cheddar and gooseberry puree.

Then lay the final layer of spinach and onion and top with Wensleydale and cranberry, with a sprinkling of grated nutmeg and the Worcestershire sauce.

Use the remaining pastry to make the lid for the pie. Seal the edges and decorate the top with any leftover pastry trimmings. Wash the top with the egg.

Bake in the centre of the oven for 45 to 50 minutes until golden brown. Allow the pie to cool for at least 40 minutes and serve at room temperature with a glass of chilled dry cider.

SERVES 6 TO 8

Veal and Ham Pie

A favourite at the Aidensfield Arms and in many other pubs and inns throughout the land.

450g / 1lb minced veal
150g / 5oz York ham, minced
1 tbsp parsley, chopped
4 tbsp cranberry jelly
grated rind of 1 lemon
2 onions, finely chopped
salt
freshly milled black pepper

Pastry
150g / 5oz lard
200ml / 7 fl oz hot water
350g / 12oz plain flour, seasoned with 1/2tsp salt
1 large egg yolk
4 eggs, hard-boiled and shelled
3 tbsp powdered aspic jelly
300ml / 10 fl oz clear apple juice (warmed)

Grease a 1.4 litre loaf tin, and line with greaseproof paper.

Pre-heat the oven to gas mark 4, 180°C / 350°F

Put the veal, ham, parsley, cranberry jelly, lemon rind and onions into a large mixing bowl. Add 1 teaspoon salt and some freshly milled black pepper. Mix all the ingredients and place to one side.

To make the pastry:

Put the lard and water into a saucepan and heat gently until the lard has melted. Bring to the boil, remove from the heat and beat in the seasoned flour to form a soft dough. Beat the egg yolk into the dough then cover the dough with a damp cloth and rest it in a warm place for 15 minutes. Do not allow the dough to cool. Roll out the pastry and pat two-thirds of it into the base and sides of the tin, evenly distribute it, to make the shape for the pie filling.

Add half the meat followed by the hardboiled eggs. Cover with the remaining meat mixture. Make a lid with the remaining pastry. Cover the pie and seal the edges. Make a large hole in the centre of the pie. Bake for 90 minutes and allow to cool for 3 hours.

Make up the aspic jelly with apple juice, cool for 10 minutes, then pour the aspic through the hole in the top of the pie. Chill the pie for 2 to 3 hours, then remove the pie from the tin.

Slice with a warm carving knife and serve with pickles and a red cabbage salad.

SERVES 8

Chicken and Ham Pie

I make two versions of this pie, one using button mushrooms and the other using florets of fresh broccoli.

25g / 1oz butter
2 carrots, diced
10 button onions, skinned
225g / 8oz York ham, shredded
25g / 1oz plain wholemeal flour
450ml / 15 fl oz milk
450g / 1lb cooked chicken breasts, cut into strips
2 tbsp double cream
salt
freshly milled black pepper
1 tsp freshly chopped tarragon
275g / 10oz puff pastry (see page 91)

Pre-heat the oven to gas mark 6, 200°C / 400°F.

Melt the butter in a saucepan and lightly fry the carrots, onions and ham for 5 minutes. Blend in the flour and cook for 1 minute. Slowly add the milk, stirring continuously until the sauce thickens and becomes smooth, then simmer for 3 minutes.

Add the chicken and cream, seasoning with salt and freshly milled black pepper.

Add the fresh tarragon.

Pour the chicken mixture into a 1.1 litre / 2 pint pie dish.

Roll out the puff pastry to form a lid to fit the pie dish, sealing the edges. Brush the top with a little milk.

Bake for 25-30 minutes until golden brown and serve with buttered broccoli and minted new potatoes.

SERVES 6

Stand Pie

There is nothing whatsoever to the rumour that this pie must be eaten standing up but, in Heartbeat country, Stand pie is always consumed in vast quantities at the country fair. For the raised crust pastry, use the same ingredients as in veal and ham pie on the previous page.

450g / 1 lb lean minced beef
225g / 8oz bacon, chopped
1 tsp fresh sage, finely chopped
pinch of mixed herbs
1 onion, finely chopped
4 tbsp oatmeal
2 tbsp brandy
3 hard-boiled eggs, shelled

Mix all the ingredients except the hard-boiled eggs in a large bowl.

Make the pastry as in the veal and ham pie, (see page 82).

SERVES 6

Venison Pasty

*Greengrass makes his venison pasties with
the meat he slices off for himself before selling
on the venison haunches to the Aidensfield Arms
and the King's Head.*

*450g / 1lb of venison, roughly minced
1 onion, finely chopped
1 bay leaf
2 sprigs fresh parsley
8 juniper berries
300ml / 10 fl oz dry red wine
25g / 1oz butter
1 tbsp cooking oil
3 tbsp redcurrant jelly
225g / 8oz potatoes, cooked and diced
salt
freshly milled black pepper
450g / 1lb shortcrust pastry (see page 91)
an egg beaten with a little milk*

Put the venison into a large shallow dish and add the
onion, bay leaf, parsley, juniper berries and wine.
Blend, cover and marinade for 4 hours.

Remove the venison from the marinade. Heat the
butter and oil in a large frying pan and fry the
venison for 5 minutes.

Strain the marinade into the pan with the venison
and reduce the marinade by half, simmering for 30
minutes until the venison is just moist and not
covered with sauce.

Add the jelly and potatoes, season well, then take
off the heat and allow to cool.

Roll out the pastry to 5mm / ¼ inch thickness
and cut out eight 15cm / 6 inch rounds.

Strain the venison mixture and divide equally
amongst the pastry rounds. Dampen the edges of
each round and fold over to make a half moon shape.
Pinch and crimp the edges. Glaze with the beaten egg
and put the pasties onto a greased baking sheet.

Bake at gas mark 4, 180°C / 350°F for 35 minutes.

Serve with some cranberry sauce and a crisp
vegetable salad.

SERVES 6-8

Aidensfield Tattie Pie

*Served with black-eyed peas at all the
bonfire parties in Aidensfield.*

*25g / 1oz beef dripping
675g / 1½lb roughly minced beef
900g / 2lb potatoes, peeled and diced
150g / 5oz carrot, diced
225g / 8oz onion, sliced
1 tbsp mixed herbs
25g / 1oz plain flour
100g / 4oz marrowfat peas
300ml / 10 fl oz beef stock
salt
freshly milled black pepper
pastry as for game pie (see page 90)
fresh milk to glaze*

Pre-heat the oven to gas mark 6, 200°C / 400°F.

Heat the dripping in a large saucepan until it is
quite hot, add the mince and quickly seal and brown
it for 5 minutes. Add the potatoes, carrot, onion and
mixed herbs, cooking for 4 minutes. Sprinkle with
the flour, stir, add the peas and beef stock, bring to
the boil and simmer for 15 minutes. Season with salt
and freshly milled black pepper. Put the mixture into
a 1.1 litre / 2 pint pie dish.

Make up the pastry as for game pie.

Trim off any excess pastry and decorate with
pastry leaves.

Brush with milk and bake in the centre of the
oven for 30-45 minutes.

SERVES 6-8

Grouse Pie

In Yorkshire, roast grouse is always served with fried bread and rowan jelly, so I have combined these ingredients to make this traditional grouse pie.

1 tbsp cooking oil
25g / 1oz butter
1lb / 16oz grouse meat
salt
freshly milled black pepper
6 slices rindless streaky bacon, finely chopped
8 shallots, peeled and sliced
1 small carrot, diced
85ml / 3 fl oz red wine
150ml / 5 fl oz chicken stock
2 tbsp double cream
5 tbsp rowan jelly (see page 131)
2 tbsp fresh parsley
275g / 10oz puff pastry (see page 91)
2 slices of white bread cut into quarters
25g / 1oz olive oil & 25g / 1oz butter

Pre-heat the oven to gas mark 6, 200°C / 400°F.

Melt the butter with the cooking oil in a large saucepan, add the grouse meat and seal the meat. Season with salt and pepper and simmer for 3 minutes. Add the bacon, shallots and carrot, stirring briskly for a further 3 minutes. Add the wine and chicken stock, bring to the boil and simmer for 25 minutes on a low heat, reducing the stock by at least one third.

Allow the grouse and sauce to cool slightly and blend in the double cream and rowan jelly.

Roll out the pastry to fit a 1.1 litre/ 2 pint pie dish.

Place the mixture into the pie dish, sprinkle with freshly chopped parsley and place on the puff pastry lid. Wash the top with a little milk and bake in the centre of the oven for 25 minutes.

Fry the bread in the hot oil and butter and place around the pie when it is ready to be served.

SERVES 4-6

Gina's Apple and Blackberry Pie

When picking apples in Yorkshire, folk always leave two on the tree for good luck – this also helps to feed the birds! The blackberries must be ripe but firm. Wash them gently under a spray of cold water.

450g / 1lb shortcrust pastry (see page 91)
450g / 1lb apples, peeled, quartered and cored
450g / 1lb blackberries, washed and hulled
100g / 4oz soft brown sugar
6 cloves, crushed
1 tsp cinnamon
1 egg white, whisked
25g / 1oz caster sugar

Pre-heat the oven to gas mark 6, 200°C / 400°F.

Line a large pie dish with two thirds of the pastry, reserving the remaining third for the lid.

Place the apples, blackberries, sugar, cloves and cinnamon into the pie dish.

Cover the pie with the remaining pastry, sealing the edges. Make a small hole in the centre of the pastry.

Brush with the egg white and sprinkle with castor sugar.

Bake for 20 minutes, then reduce the heat to gas mark 4, 180°C / 350°F and bake for a further 20 minutes.

Remove from the oven allow to cool for 10 minutes. Serve with whipped double cream.

SERVES 8

Fish Pie

This recipe contains salmon or haddock poached in a creamy sauce, topped with creamed potatoes. Serve this with baked parsnips and mange tout to make an excellent meal.

450g / 1lb salmon or haddock fillets, skinned
100g / 4oz spring onions, finely chopped
1 tbsp lemon juice
100g / 4oz button mushrooms, sliced
1 bay leaf
300ml / 10 fl oz milk
25g / 1oz unsalted butter
25g / 1oz seasoned flour
450g / 1lb cooked potatoes, mashed with 25g / 1oz butter and 2 tbsp double cream
100g / 4oz Wensleydale cheese, grated

Pre-heat the oven to gas mark 5, 190°C / 375°F.

Place the salmon or haddock, onions, lemon juice, mushrooms and bay leaf into a saucepan. Pour the milk over and slowly bring to the boil.

Cover and simmer for 15 minutes. Carefully remove the fish and vegetables, strain the liquid into a bowl and reserve. Discard any fish bones with the bay leaf.

Melt the butter in a saucepan, gradually adding the flour. Cook gently for 2 minutes, then slowly add the reserved milk. Bring to the boil and simmer for 2 minutes until the sauce thickens and becomes very smooth. Add the fish and vegetables.

Place the mixture into a shallow 1.1 litre / 2 pint ovenproof serving dish. Allow the mixture to cool and then cover completely with creamed mashed potato, sprinkle all over with the grated cheese and bake in the centre of the oven for 30 minutes until golden brown.

SERVES 4

Yorkshire Mint Pasties

The ingredients for the mint pasty are very similar to those used in Eccles cakes, Chorley cakes and Newburgh cakes from Lancashire.

225g / 8oz shortcrust pastry
25g / 1oz butter
100g / 4oz currants
25g / 1oz mixed peel
50g / 2oz mixed fruit
50g / 2oz demerara sugar
½ tsp mixed spice
½ tsp freshly grated ginger
½ tsp freshly grated nutmeg
3 tbsp of freshly chopped mint

Pre-heat the oven to gas mark 7, 220°C / 425°F

Melt the butter in a saucepan, add all the ingredients and allow the mixture to simmer for 4 minutes. Then let it cool.

Roll out the pastry, then with a 15cm / 6 inch cutter, cut out the pastry into rounds.

Put a generous tablespoon of the mixture into the centre, dampen the edges and fold over to form a half moon shape. Seal the edges, lightly brush with a little milk and place the patties onto a greased baking sheet.

Bake in the centre of the oven for 15-20 minutes until golden brown.

Serve with Wensleydale cheese and a glass of port.

SERVES 4

Game Pie

These days you can buy a selection of game meat from the supermarket or your local butcher. Traditional game pie should be topped with a puff pastry crust but I am going to make it using my own shortcrust pastry specially devised for this recipe.

50g/ 2oz butter
50g / 2oz dripping or lard
775g / 1½ lb of mixed game meat: venison, rabbit and pheasant, bones and fat removed.
225g / 8oz button mushrooms
225g / 8oz shallots, peeled
2 cloves garlic
3 tbsp seasoned plain flour
300ml / 10 fl oz claret
300ml / 10 fl oz beef stock
1 onion, chopped
8 juniper berries
pinch of allspice
pinch of fresh marjoram
1 tsp salt
freshly milled black pepper

Pastry
175g / 6oz plain flour
50g / 2oz shredded suet
4 tbsp cold water blended with 1 egg yolk
pinch of salt
freshly ground black pepper
75g / 3oz unsalted butter, softened

Add the fat into a very large saucepan and heat gently. Add the game and seal the meat by cooking for 5 minutes.

Add the mushroom, shallots and garlic, cooking for a further 4 minutes. Sprinkle with the flour and cook for 3 minutes. Slowly add the wine and beef stock. Add the rest of the ingredients and cook for a few minutes and allow to come to the boil. Take the pan from the heat and allow to stand for 6 hours.

Make up the pastry by sifting the flour into a mixing bowl, adding the suet, salt and freshly milled black pepper. Blend in the butter with your fingertips, and when the mixture resembles fine breadcrumbs, add the water and egg, binding into a stiff dough.

Knead the dough lightly for 4 minutes, then cover and leave in a warm place until required.

Bring the game mix to the boil and simmer, reducing the stock by half. Place the cooked meat and the sauce into a 1.1 litre / 2 pint pie dish .

Roll out the pastry and cover the pie dish, sealing the edges. Coat with a little milk and bake in the centre of the oven for 50 minutes at gas mark 4, 180°C / 350°F.

Serve with rowan jelly and creamed potatoes.

SERVES 6-8

Yorkshire Shortcrust Pastry

Good pastry should always be light and crumbly so it is important to weigh all the ingredients accurately and keep the utensils and your hands as cool as possible.

350g / 12oz plain flour
½ tsp salt
75g / 3oz butter
75g / 3oz lard
flour for rolling

Sift the flour and salt into a clean bowl, then gently rub in the butter and lard until the mixture resembles fine breadcrumbs.

Add enough cold water to make a stiff dough. Press the dough together with your fingertips.

Roll the pastry out on a lightly floured surface. Use as directed in the recipes.

Puff Pastry

When making puff pastry, make a large batch and freeze half of it because the process is long and time consuming. The pastry will keep for up to three months in the freezer.

225g / 8oz plain flour
¼ tsp salt
225g / 8oz butter
½ tsp lemon juice
flour for rolling

Sift the flour and salt into a clean mixing bowl. Gently rub in 50g / 2oz of the butter. Add the lemon juice and a little cold water to make a smooth dough.

Shape the remaining butter into a rectangle on a sheet of greaseproof paper.

Carefully roll out the dough on a lightly floured surface to a strip a little wider than the butter and twice its size in length.

Place the butter on one half of the pastry and gently fold over the other half, pressing the edges with the floured rolling pin.

Leave the pastry in a cool place for 20 minutes to allow the butter to harden.

Roll out the pastry on a lightly floured surface. Fold the bottom third up and the top third down, pressing the edges together with the rolling pin. Turn the pastry so the folded edges are on the right and left of you. Roll and fold again, cover and leave in a cool place for 15 minutes. Repeat this process of rolling out six times.

The pastry is now ready for use.

Chapter 8
Game Recipes

The Glorious Twelfth of August is a popular date among the many moorland farmers around Yorkshire who seek out the red grouse for their tables, to serve with the traditional bread sauce. Game brings out the best in Claude Greengrass, a prize-winning poacher of pheasant, partridge and grouse. It's at this time of year that PC Rowan and Sergeant Blaketon can be found patrolling the woods around Allerston and Danby, finding out if any of these game birds have accidentally fallen out of the skies and hurt themselves.

ROAST MOOR BIRD WITH
BREAD SAUCE

SERGEANT BLAKETON'S
BREAST OF DUCKLING IN
HONEY AND LEMON

AIDENSFIELD BREAST OF
WILD DUCK WITH WHISKY,
RASPBERRY AND HONEY
SAUCE

MARMALIZED BREAST OF
DUCKLING

GREENGRASS ON RABBIT
CASSEROLES

PHEASANT WITH BABY
ONIONS AND PEAS

BREAST OF PARTRIDGE WITH
SPINACH AND MUSHROOMS
WITH A WHITE WINE AND
RED CHERRY SAUCE

JUGGED HARE WITH
GROUSE AND POTATO AND
HERB DUMPLINGS

CLAUDE GREENGRASS ON
ROAST DUCKLING

Roast Moor Bird with Bread Sauce

In Yorkshire, grouse is known as the moor bird, and the only way to serve it is with bread sauce. PC Phil Bellamy loves his grouse with bread sauce.

4 oven ready grouse
50g / 2oz butter
juice of 1 lemon
225g / 8oz redcurrants or cranberries
salt
freshly milled black pepper
8 rashers of streaky bacon
pinch thyme

Pre-heat the oven to gas mark 6, 200°C / 400°F.

Gently melt the butter in a saucepan. Add the lemon juice, redcurrants or cranberries, with a sprinkle of salt and freshly milled black pepper. Cook for 1 minute and allow to cool.

Fill the cavities of each bird with the currants and juice, seasoning the birds all over with salt and freshly milled black pepper.

Wrap 2 slices of streaky bacon over each breast. Sprinkle with thyme.

Wrap each bird in some greased foil and place them breast down in a roasting tin. Roast for 15 minutes then remove the foil and roast for a further 10 minutes.

Serve with bread sauce.

SERVES 4

Sergeant Blaketon's Breast of Duckling Cooked in Honey and Lemon

'Greengrass generously sold me these duck breasts. What he did with the legs I am sure can be written down to make another recipe.'

4 x 175g / 6oz duck breast
50g / 2oz butter
4 tbsp white rum
150g / 5oz raisins
2 tbsp clear honey
1 tbsp tarragon vinegar
2 lemons, juice and zest
150ml / ¼ pint sour cream or fromage frais
salt
freshly milled black pepper

Cut the breast fillets into thin slices, each weighing 25g / 1oz, giving 6 per serving.

Heat the butter in a frying pan, add the duck and cook gently for 8 minutes, turning frequently until the breasts are lightly coloured. Add the lemon and honey and cook for a further 5 minutes.

Remove from the pan and arrange in a round spiral shape on a large serving plate and keep warm.

Return the juices from the duck to the pan and heat. Add the vinegar and raisins and simmer for 2 minutes. Season with salt and freshly milled black pepper, add the rum and cook for a further 3 minutes. Finally add the cream until the sauce is reduced by half. Pour the sauce into the centre of the duck spiral and serve immediately.

SERVES 4

Aidensfield Breast of Wild Duck with Whisky, Raspberry and Honey Sauce

This recipe originally appeared on the menu at the Brewers Arms and is now a firm favourite throughout Yorkshire.

4 duckling breasts, skin on
150ml / 5 fl oz Beef stock
salt
freshly milled black pepper
25g / 1oz butter
25g / 1oz flour
4 tbsp honey
4 tbsp whisky liquor
100g / 4oz fresh or frozen raspberries
50g / 2oz carrot, finely chopped
50g / 2oz shallots, finely chopped
1 tbsp lemon juice
1 tbsp Worcestershire sauce

Trim and score the duck breast. Season well all over.

Put the butter into the frying pan and fry the duck breasts skin side first.

Add the chopped carrot, lemon juice and a little of the beef stock.

Add the whisky liquor and let it simmer for one minute, then add a little honey, a few raspberries and a sprinkle of flour.

Allow to cook for a few minutes, seasoning with freshly ground black pepper. Add the Worcestershire sauce.

Repeat the process, adding the beef stock and honey, allowing 3 minutes cooking time.

Remove the duck breasts from the pan but allow the sauce to continue simmering.

Slice the duck breast lengthways into ½cm / ¼ inch pieces.

Pour a little of the sauce onto the serving plate arrange the duck breast into a fan shape and decorate with fresh raspberries and a slice of lemon.

SERVES 4

Marmalized Breast of Duckling

Mrs Pinkerton gave Greengrass this recipe in exchange for some duck legs!

4 duck breasts
85g / 3oz thick cut marmalade
85g / 3oz blackcurrants
225g / 8oz shallots, peeled and sliced
120ml / 4 fl oz port
30ml / 1 fl oz brandy
1 tbsp red wine vinegar
1 tsp pink peppercorns
freshly milled black pepper
salt
30g / 1oz unsalted butter
30ml / 1 fl oz olive oil

Pre-heat the oven to gas mark 8, 230°C / 450°F.

Heat the oil and butter in a roasting pan.

Season and sear the duck breasts with a sharp knife.

Quickly fry the duck breasts over a high heat until lightly brown. Drain.

Place all the ingredients into a large bowl, blend thoroughly.

Heavily coat the breasts with the marmalade mixture and cook in the oven for 20 minutes, basting every 5 minutes with the marinade.

Remove the duck breasts and slice each one into 8 slices lengthways, keeping them warm on a serving tray in a low oven.

Put the marinade from the duck and any mixture that is left into a saucepan and reduce the marmalade sauce over a high heat until it is of a thick consistency.

Pour the sauce over the slices of duck, grill for 1 minute and serve.

SERVES 4

Rabbit Casseroles

Rabbit and hare were always country favourites, but are less popular today. Try this recipe for an authentic taste of tradition!

100g / 4oz rindless streaky bacon
900g / 2lb rabbit or hare, skinned, cleaned and jointed
4 potatoes, peeled and chopped
3 onions, sliced
2 carrots, sliced
100g / 4oz mushrooms, quartered
1 tsp thyme
1 tbsp parsley
salt
freshly milled black pepper
600ml / 20 fl oz / 1 pint chicken stock
15ml / 1 tbsp cornflour blended with a little wine

Pre-heat the oven to gas mark 3, 170°C / 325°F

Trim the bacon, cutting each rasher into 5 or 6 pieces.

Layer a casserole with the rabbit, bacon and vegetables.

Sprinkle with the herbs, seasoning well with salt and freshly milled black pepper.

Pour over the stock and cook for 2 hours.

Thicken the casserole with the cornflour and wine mixture and serve with red cabbage and thick crusty bread.

SERVES 4

Pheasant with Baby Onions and Green Peas

A traditional Yorkshire dish that dates back over two centuries.

2 large pheasants
50g / 2oz butter
25g / 1oz plain flour
225g / 8oz pork fat, cut into small cubes
16 small onions or shallots, peeled
600ml / 20 fl oz chicken stock
450g / 1lb shelled fresh peas
bouquet garni
salt
freshly milled black pepper

Pre-heat the oven to gas mark 6, 200°C / 400°F.

Place the pork fat into a pan of boiling salted water and simmer for three minutes. Drain and dry.

Melt the butter in a large frying pan, add the pork and onions, browning lightly for 3 minutes.

Remove the pork and onions from the pan and set aside. Place the pheasants in the frying pan and brown them all over. Remove them from the pan and place on a baking tray.

Add the flour to the pan, cook until it begins to brown, then slowly blend in the chicken stock.

Cook the pheasants in the oven for 45 minutes with the sauce and bouquet garni.

Remove the bouquet garni 10 minutes before the end of cooking and add the onions, pork and peas.

When cooked, place the pheasants on a large platter and surround with the pork, peas, onions and gravy.

SERVES 4

100

Breast of Partridge with Spinach and Mushrooms with a White Wine and Red Cherry Sauce

The heart will beat a little faster when you sample Greengrass's favourite bird. He sells partridge at Thackerston, Bransford and Ryedale to make himself some beer money.

8 partridge breasts

Stuffing

3 shallots, peeled and finely chopped
50g / 2oz butter
125g / 4oz button mushroom, thinly sliced
75g / 3oz spinach, cooked
1 tbsp chervil
2 tbsp cointreau

Sauce

25g / 1oz butter
2 shallots, chopped
150ml / ¼ pint chicken stock
75g / 3oz fresh cherries, stoned and peeled
150ml / ¼ pint of white wine
50g / 2oz button mushrooms, sliced
150ml / ¼ pint of fromage frais
1 tbsp cherry brandy
salt
freshly milled black pepper

Pre-heat the oven to gas mark 6, 200°C / 400°F.

Sauté the chopped shallots in the butter, add the mushrooms and cook for 2 minutes. Add the spinach, season and cook for a further minute. Finally add the chervil and cointreau. Blend and allow to cool.

Slice the partridge breast inwards to make a pocket, fill each breast with the stuffing.

Butter the breast and wrap them in foil and cook in the oven for 20 minutes. While they are cooking, make the sauce.

Sauté the cherries, shallots and mushroom in butter for 3 minutes. Add the white wine and chicken stock and reduce by three quarters. Add the fromage frais and cherry brandy. Season and reduce by half.

Serve this sauce in a sauceboat, garnished with fresh cherries

SERVES 4

Jugged Hare
with Grouse and Potato Herb Dumplings

This was once known as 'poor man's pie', but it was revived in the sixties when the price of hare had rocketed. Now we can simply call it 'rich man's pie'.

50g / 2oz butter
75g / 3oz streaky bacon, chopped
675g / 1½lb Hare meat or 1 large hare, jointed
350g / 12oz grouse meat
1 onion, chopped
2 carrots, peeled and diced
2 sticks celery, chopped
salt
freshly milled black pepper
rind of ½ lemon
900ml / 30 fl oz chicken stock
25g / 1oz plain flour
5 tbsp port

Potato Herb Dumplings
350g / 12oz mashed potato
1 egg, beaten
salt
freshly milled black pepper
a generous pinch of mixed herbs
50g / 2oz seasoned flour
25g / 1oz semolina
2 tbsp milk

Place all the ingredients for the dumplings into a bowl and mix thoroughly. Shape into small balls and place to one side until required.

Add the butter and bacon to a large saucepan and cook for 3 minutes. Add the hare and grouse and simmer for 7 minutes until the game is browned. Add the vegetables and lemon rind, seasoning well with salt and freshly milled black pepper.

Pour over the meat, bring to the boil and simmer for 3 hours on a low heat.

Mix the flour with a little port to make a paste and add to the hare. Cook for 3 minutes, then add the rest of the port.

Add the dumplings, cover and simmer for a further 20 minutes.

Serve with some crusty bread and a bottle of dry red wine.

SERVES APPROX 6

Claude Greengrass on Roast Duckling

...and how to cook it 'What I don't know about ducks is not worth talking about !' If you buy duckling, do try to buy fresh. If you buy a frozen one then thaw the duckling overnight at room temperature.

Pre-heat the oven to gas mark 4, 180°C / 350°F. Remove the giblets and wash the duckling. Prick all over with a fork and rub a little salt into the skin. Place a grill rack or trivet into a baking tray and place the duckling on top to allow the fat to run away from it.

Roast in the centre of the oven without basting. Allow 35 minutes per 450g / 1lb. Roast until the skin is crisp and golden.

Before the last 30 minutes of cooking time, coat the duckling with honey or marmalade, turn the oven up to gas mark 6, 200°C / 400°F.

Chapter 9

Winter Warmers

Fires burning in the grate, friends coming to visit on a cold winter's night – all these things make the Yorkshire moors glow with warmth. When the snow falls, chaos is brought to the roads, so PC Nick Rowan will need his flask of hot soup to keep him going through the night, pulling cars, sheep and cattle out of snowdrifts. Back at the station Sergeant Blaketon reads the Daily Sketch while listening to the Spencer Davies Group sing 'Keep on Running' on the radio. While all this is going on, Claude Greengrass will be snuggled up in his lodgings with a rum toddy and poacher's pie, thinking about his next pint of Yorkshire bitter.

OXTAIL SOUP WITH
TARRAGON DUMPLINGS

CHICKEN AND LEEK SOUP

SERGEANT BLAKETON'S
WINTER WARMER

LIVER, BACON AND
ONION BAKE

YORKSHIRE MIST

PEA AND HAM BROTH

ROBIN HOOD'S BAY
CRAB SOUP

YORKSHIRE OVEN
BOTTOM CAKE

ROAST LAMB WITH
ROSEMARY AND HONEY
SAUCE

GREENGRASS'S
POACHER'S PIE

BAKED TROUT WITH
ALMONDS AND DILL

ROAST SIRLOIN WITH
HERB STUFFING

Oxtail Soup with Fresh Tarragon Dumplings

With several tinned varieties of oxtail soup available on the market, the original taste of real oxtail soup is unknown to most of us. The combination of fresh oxtails and tarragon dumplings is something that every lover of good British food should experience at least once in their lives. This recipe is made in two stages, but I am sure you will find it worth the extra effort.

Stage One:
1 whole oxtail
50g / 2oz seasoned plain flour
100g / 4oz butter
1.5 litres / 3 pints beef stock
3 tbsp sunflower oil
1 large carrot
1 stick of celery
1 onion
small turnip
1 tsp thyme
1 bay leaf
110ml / 4 fl oz claret or sherry
salt
freshly ground black pepper

Stage Two: Tarragon Dumplings
50g / 2oz self-raising flour
50g / 2oz fresh breadcrumbs
2 tbsp shredded suet
2 tbsp fresh tarragon leaves
2 tbsp finely grated lemon rind
1 egg
salt
freshly ground black pepper

Chop the oxtail into pieces, coating lightly with the seasoned flour.

Quickly fry in hot butter in a large deep saucepan until they are lightly browned.

Peel and dice all the vegetables into 2.5cm / 1 inch squares.

Add the oil to the pan and brown them together. Pour over the claret and add all the rest of the ingredients except the beef stock.

Cook for 10 minutes, then gradually add the beef stock. Simmer for three hours, skimming of any excess fat. Strain off the liquid into large clean saucepan and allow it to cool.

Remove the oxtail meat and chop it finely, returning it to the soup. Re-boil and adjust the seasoning. Allow to simmer while making the dumplings.

To make the tarragon dumplings, mix together all the dry ingredients in a large clean bowl. Add the egg and blend in thoroughly. Add enough milk to make the dough moist, shape into small balls, roll them in a little flour and cook them for 10 minutes in boiling salted water. Remove them carefully and add them to the soup. Cook for a further 12 minutes, then serve with a home-made crusty bread.

SERVES 6-8

Author's tip: Mash the leftover vegetables with a little butter, shape them into little patties, dip them into some seasoned flour and fry them in butter. Serve them with your main course.

Chicken and Leek Soup

This is a main course soup and was originally made with beef and chicken. To add some colour to the soup, why not throw in a handful of chopped red peppers?

30g/ 1oz butter
350g / 12oz uncooked chicken meat, bones removed
350g / 12oz leeks, washed and cut into 2.5cm / 1 inch pieces
1.1 litres / 2 pints chicken stock
bouquet garni
salt
freshly milled white pepper
8 prunes, stoned and halved

Melt the butter in a large saucepan and fry the chicken and leeks for 8 minutes.

Add the stock and bouquet garni, seasoning well to taste.

Bring the soup to the boil and simmer for 45 minutes.

Add the prunes with the diced peppers if you wish, and simmer for 20 minutes.

Serve with croutons.

SERVES 6

Sergeant Blaketon's Winter Warmer

A fish soup to keep out the cold on the rawest of November nights!

350g / 12oz haddock, skinned
350g / 12oz cod fillet
600ml / 1 pint of milk
600ml / 1 pint of water
450g / 1lb cooked potatoes, sliced
225g / 8oz sliced onions
100g / 4oz peas
25g / 1oz butter
salt
freshly milled black pepper

Place the fish into a large saucepan, cover with boiling water and simmer for 6 minutes.

Remove any bones from the fish and boil for a further 20 minutes.

Flake the haddock and the cod. Strain the stock adding the milk, potatoes, onions, peas and the flaked fish. Simmer for 25 minutes, adjusting the seasoning. Add the butter and garnish with parsley. Serve with crusty wholemeal bread.

SERVES 6

Liver, Bacon and Onion Bake

If you've got to go and help dig sheep out of the snow you'll need some of this to set you up, and don't forget to take some Yorkshire Mist (next recipe) in your thermos!

8 smoked streaky bacon rashers, rindless and chopped
350g / 12oz lamb's liver, finely sliced
25g / 1oz best dripping
450g / 1lb King Edward potatoes, sliced
450g / 1lb onions, chopped
600ml / 1 pint beef stock
salt
freshly milled black pepper
freshly chopped parsley
100g / 4oz grated cheese

Melt the dripping in a large frying pan and cook the bacon and liver for 8 minutes. In a separate pan fry the potatoes and onions for 12 minutes.

Place the liver and bacon into an ovenproof casserole dish, top with the potatoes and onion.

Add enough stock just to reach the potato base.

Season and sprinkle with parsley and grated cheese.

Bake in the oven at gas mark 6, 200°C / 400°F for 25 minutes.

SERVES 4

Yorkshire Mist

A foggy night in Castleton was the inspiration for this thick misty soup.

450g / 1lb leeks, trimmed, sliced and washed
25g / 1oz butter
350g / 12oz Spanish onions, chopped
2 celery sticks, chopped
2 tbsp rice
2tbsp split peas
1.2lt / 2 pints lamb stock
salt
freshly milled black pepper
100ml / 4 fl oz double cream
chives

Melt the butter in a large saucepan, add the leeks, onion and celery and cook gently for 10 minutes.

Add the rice, split peas and lamb stock, simmering for 40 minutes.

Season to taste, reheat and serve with chopped chives, chunky bread or warm oatcakes (see page 63).

SERVES 4-6

Pea and Ham Broth

Use only authentic York ham for this soup. To add an extra something to this recipe, add the tarragon dumplings from the recipe on page 106.

3 rashers of smoked, rindless streaky bacon, diced
1 large onion, chopped
small knob of butter
450g / 1lb soaked peas
225g / 8oz York ham, cubed
2.3 ltr / 4 pints of chicken stock
salt
freshly milled black pepper
150ml / 5 fl oz double cream
chopped parsley
croutons

Put the bacon and onion into a large saucepan with a little butter and cook over a gentle heat for 6 minutes.

Add the peas, ham and the stock to the pan, bring to the boil, season lightly with salt and freshly milled black pepper, cover and simmer for 2 hours.

Add the cream and blend thoroughly, sprinkle with parsley and top with cheesy croutons.

SERVES 4-6

Robin Hood's Bay Crab Soup

Robin Hood's Bay is quite near to Whitby. It's on the edge of Heartbeat country and is well worth a visit.

225g/ 8oz fresh crab meat
1 large onion, sliced
1.2lt / 2 pints fish stock
50g / 2oz butter
25g / 1oz plain flour
grated rind and juice of 1 orange
275ml / ½ pint double cream
50ml / 2 fl oz dry sherry
1 tbsp anchovy essence
salt
freshly milled black pepper

Melt the butter in a large saucepan, add the onion and crab meat and cook gently for 6 minutes. Add the flour, stirring thoroughly to avoid lumps. Very slowly add the fish stock, stirring all the time, until the soup comes to the boil. Simmer for 40 minutes.

Season with salt and freshly milled black pepper, adding the anchovy essence, orange juice, rind, sherry and cream.

Re-heat and serve with brown crusty bread and a dry white wine.

SERVES 4-6

Yorkshire Oven Bottom Cake

The next best thing to sliced bread, I always say! Although delicious when sliced into generous chunks to accompany soups and winter warmers, Yorkshire oven bottom cakes are also good spread with garlic butter or soaked with gravy.

1.5 kg / 3lb strong plain white flour
25g / 1oz salt
25g / 1oz lard
25g / 1oz fresh yeast, mixed with 1 tsp sugar
and 900ml warm water
100g / 4oz lard, cut into 24 pieces

Pre-heat the oven gas mark 7, 220°C / 425°F.

Sieve the flour and salt into a large bowl, rubbing in the lard with your fingertips until the mixture resembles breadcrumbs. Add the yeast mixture and blend and knead until it becomes a very firm dough.

Cover and leave in a warm area for 25 minutes.

Fold over and knead the fat into the dough. Put the dough onto a greased baking tray and score into 8 pieces, then bake for 20 minutes until golden brown.

SERVES 8

Roast Lamb with Rosemary and Honey Sauce

Alternatively, try this recipe with sage and marmalade smeared on the lamb.

3lb / 1 leg of lamb, boned and rolled
salt
freshly milled black pepper
2 cloves garlic, crushed
1 tsp paprika
3 sprigs of rosemary, soaked in 6 tbsp fresh orange juice
6 tbsp clear honey
1 tbsp of freshly chopped mint
150ml / 5 fl oz beef stock
1 tbsp of cornflour mixed with a little orange juice

Pre-heat the oven to gas mark 6, 200°C / 400°F.

Rub the lamb with the salt, pepper, garlic and paprika and cook in the oven for 30 minutes.

Place the rest of the ingredients except the cornflour into a saucepan and bring to the boil. Simmer for 15 minutes.

Thicken with the cornflour.

Baste the lamb with the rosemary and honey sauce every 15 minutes for 1 hour.

Place the lamb on a large serving plate, carve then add the juices to the rest of the rosemary and honey sauce.

Serve with the sauce, new potatoes and fresh winter cabbage.

SERVES 4 TO 6

Greengrass's Poacher's Pie

This pie is quite different from the game pie recipe on page 90.

225g / 8oz boneless rabbit, skinned and cubed
225g / 8oz boneless grouse, skin removed and cubed
225g / 8oz boneless pheasant, skin removed and cubed
100g / 4oz rindless streaky bacon, chopped
1 large leek, sliced and washed
2 potatoes, sliced
1 tbsp freshly chopped parsley
pinch of thyme
chicken stock

Pastry
225g / 8oz plain flour
salt
freshly milled white pepper
50g / 2oz butter
50g / 2oz lard
1 egg to glaze

Pre-heat the oven to gas mark 5, 190°C / 375°F.

Fill a large pie dish with layers of the game, bacon and vegetables. Season well and add the herbs and just enough chicken stock to half fill the pie dish.

To make the pastry put the flour and a little seasoning into a bowl. Rub in the butter and lard until the mixture resembles fine breadcrumbs, adding enough cold water to form a very firm dough.

Roll out enough pastry on a lightly floured surface to cover the pie dish.

Trim and seal the edges, making a small hole in the centre to let out the steam.

Brush the top with the egg.

Bake in the oven for 35 minutes. Cover loosely with greased baking foil, reducing the heat to gas mark 4, 180°C / 350°F for one hour. Serve with Yorkshire oven-bottom cake (see previous page) red cabbage and a pint of Yorkshire bitter.

SERVES 8

Baked Trout with Almonds and Dill

Trout are plentiful in Yorkshire's streams and rivers and this is one of my favourite trout recipes.

4 x 275g / 10oz salmon trout, gutted and cleaned
8 tbsp fresh lemon juice
salt
freshly milled black pepper
4 tbsp roasted almond niblets
4 sprigs of fresh dill
8 rashers of rindless, streaky bacon
150ml / 5 fl oz dry white wine
50g / 2oz butter
75g / 3oz split almonds, roasted
2 tbsp soured cream or yoghurt
4 sprigs of fresh dill for garnish
2 lemons, thinly sliced

Pre-heat the oven to gas mark 4, 180°C / 350°F.

Sprinkle 6 tablespoons of lemon juice over the cavities of the fish, seasoning inside and out with salt and freshly milled black pepper. Place a sprig of dill and a tablespoon of almonds into each cavity, then carefully seal by wrapping 2 pieces of streaky bacon around each trout. Place them into an ovenproof dish. Pour over the wine and cover the dish with greased cooking foil.

Bake in the oven for 30 minutes, the first 20 minutes in foil, then the last 10 minutes with the foil removed.

Melt the butter in a saucepan, add the almonds and the remaining lemon juice and the juices from the trout. Simmer the fish stock and reduce by half. Add 2 tablespoons of soured cream or yoghurt and simmer for 3 minutes.

Place the trout onto serving plates, spoon over the sauce and garnish with a fresh sprig of dill and slices of lemon.

SERVES 4

Roast Sirloin with Herb Stuffing and Yorkshire Pudding

Knighted in Lancashire it may have been, but the Sir-Loin of beef is not a recipe to be left out of any good cookbook.

25g / 1oz beef dripping
4 shallots, roughly chopped
50g / 2oz wild mushrooms, finely chopped
1 tsp of dried tarragon
1 tsp of dried parsley
50g / 2oz fresh brown breadcrumbs
2 sprigs of fresh thyme
salt
freshly milled black pepper
1 egg, blended with 1 tbsp port
2 tbsp double cream
1kg / 2 lb sirloin steak, in one piece
6 potatoes, washed and pricked all over

Pre-heat the oven gas mark 6, 200°C/ 400°F.

Melt the dripping in a large saucepan and fry the shallots and mushrooms for 5 minutes. Remove the pan from the heat and blend in all the ingredients except the egg and cream.

Allow the mixture to cool, and add the remaining ingredients.

Place the steak on a board. Insert a sharp knife into the middle of the steak and slice horizontally to within 2.5cm / 1 inch of the end of the steak, making a pocket.

Place the stuffing inside the steak. Sew up the pocket with butchers string or thick cotton. Place the steak onto a large baking tray, with the potatoes supporting the meat, 3 on either side of it. Bake in the centre of the oven for 1 hour .

Place the meat onto a serving dish, remove the string and carve into generous thick slices.

Serve with Yorkshire pudding, baked parsnips, cauliflower cheese and the potatoes.

SERVES 6

Chapter 10
Aidensfield at Christmas

So that you don't spoil your appetite for the Christmas dinner buffet, I suggest you start the day with a light yet luxurious breakfast. Greengrass is quite happy just having the hair of the dog, but the rest of us can sample a Christmas treat with Kate's champagne fruit salad and smoked salmon with scrambled eggs. This should satisfy you until the evening, when you can indulge in a lavish Yorkshire feast. Set the buffet out on a table so that everybody can help themselves to a little of what they fancy.

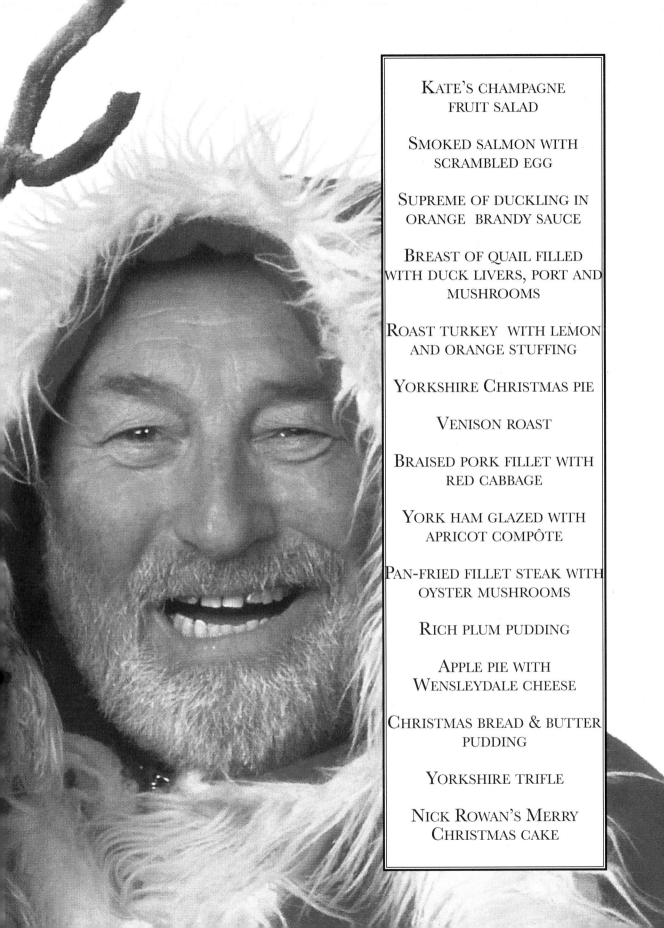

KATE'S CHAMPAGNE
FRUIT SALAD

SMOKED SALMON WITH
SCRAMBLED EGG

SUPREME OF DUCKLING IN
ORANGE BRANDY SAUCE

BREAST OF QUAIL FILLED
WITH DUCK LIVERS, PORT AND
MUSHROOMS

ROAST TURKEY WITH LEMON
AND ORANGE STUFFING

YORKSHIRE CHRISTMAS PIE

VENISON ROAST

BRAISED PORK FILLET WITH
RED CABBAGE

YORK HAM GLAZED WITH
APRICOT COMPÔTE

PAN-FRIED FILLET STEAK WITH
OYSTER MUSHROOMS

RICH PLUM PUDDING

APPLE PIE WITH
WENSLEYDALE CHEESE

CHRISTMAS BREAD & BUTTER
PUDDING

YORKSHIRE TRIFLE

NICK ROWAN'S MERRY
CHRISTMAS CAKE

Kate's Champagne Fruit Salad

If you are making this for a buffet party, simply double the quantity.

3 mandarins, peeled
1 kiwi fruit, peeled and chopped
1 banana, peeled and chopped
·1 pear, peeled, cored and diced
1 apple, peeled, cored and diced
2 plums, sliced and pitted
225g / 8oz seedless grapes, sliced
100g / 4oz fresh strawberries, hulled and sliced
2 tbsp brandy
2 tbsp lemon juice
150ml / 5 fl oz Champagne

Put all the fruit in a bowl. Add the brandy, lemon juice and champagne. Chill for 1 hour and serve in individual glass dishes with a sprig of fresh mint.

SERVES 4-6

Smoked Salmon with Scrambled Eggs

Beat 2 eggs per person and season with salt and freshly milled black pepper.

Melt a small knob of butter into a saucepan over a gentle heat and add the eggs, stirring all the time with a wooden spoon. Add 50g / 2oz smoked salmon cut into small diamonds.

Take the pan from the heat, add a little more butter with 1 tbsp double cream and serve with a sprig of freshly snipped parsley and lightly buttered warm brown toast.

Supreme of Duckling in Orange Brandy Sauce

This makes a nice change from the traditional turkey and is easier to cook.

5og / 2oz butter
2 tbsp olive oil
25g / 1oz plain flour
8 x 225g / 8oz duckling supreme
2 tbsp fresh tarragon, chopped
150ml / 5 fl oz fresh orange juice
3 fresh oranges cut into segments and rind cut into very fine strips
25g / 2oz courgettes, cut into very fine strips
25g / 2oz red peppers, cut into very fine strips
25 / 2oz leeks, shredded
150ml / 5 fl oz orange brandy
salt
freshly milled black pepper
150ml /5 fl oz fromage frais

Heat the butter and oil in a large frying pan, add the duck supremes and cook quickly until golden brown.

Add the orange brandy and cook for 2 minutes. Sprinkle lightly with the flour and cook for a further minute.

Reduce the heat and add the orange juice, courgettes, peppers and leeks. Season with salt and freshly milled black pepper and simmer for 4 minutes until the orange sauce is reduced.

Add half the orange segments, orange rind, tarragon and fromage frais cook for a further 2 minutes.

Slice the duck breasts into thin segments and fan around the centre of a large warm plate. Serve with a little sauce, garnished with the segments of orange and fresh tarragon leaves.

SERVES 8

Breast of Quail Filled with Duck Livers, Port and Mushrooms with a Cream and Honey Sauce

Garnished with holly and mistletoe, this cannot help but bring some Yorkshire Christmas cheer to the dining table.

16 quails, boned and cooked for 15 minutes
16 soft boiled quail eggs (3 minutes)
50g / 2oz butter
225g / 8oz duck livers
175g / 6oz mushrooms, chopped
175g / 6oz onions, chopped
4 tbsp port
4 tbsp dry red wine
2 tbsp warm honey
3 tbsp fromage frais
salt
freshly milled black pepper
blackcurrants

Put the butter into a large saucepan and fry the duck livers for 1 minute. Add the onion and mushrooms.

Season well with salt and freshly ground black pepper.

Add the port, red wine and quail meat and allow to simmer for 6 minutes.

Pour over the honey and fromage frais, blend and simmer for a further 2 minutes.

Garnish the warm plates with the quail eggs cut into halves with a few berries.

Place a large pastry cutter into the centre of each plate and fill it with the livers, mushroom, onion and sauce.

Remove the cutter and top the filling with quail meat and some sauce.

SERVES 8

Roast Turkey with Lemon and Orange Stuffing

Everybody enjoys turkey at Christmas, so why not try it this year with Nick's favourite St Clement's stuffing.

4.5kg / 10lb oven-ready turkey
100g / 4oz melted butter
juice of 1 lemon
juice of 1 orange
5 tbsp sweet white wine
2 tbsp freshly chopped mint

Lemon and Orange Stuffing
50g / 2oz butter
4 tbsp shallots, finely chopped
1 tbsp freshly chopped mint
500g / 1lb sausage meat
juice and finely grated rind of 2 lemons and 2 oranges
100g / 4oz fresh brown breadcrumbs
2 tbsp fresh parsley, finely chopped
salt
freshly milled black pepper
10 mini pork sausages
10 small slices of rindless streaky bacon
3 oranges
3 lemons
2 sprigs of parsley

Pre-heat the oven to gas mark 7, 220°C / 425°F.

For the lemon and orange stuffing:

Fry the shallots in the butter for 4 minutes, add the mint and cook for 1 minute.

Put all the other stuffing ingredients into a large bowl and blend together with the cooked shallots, mint and butter.

Stuff the neck end of the turkey, truss and place on a rack in a large roasting tin. Place in the oven.

Put the butter, lemon, orange, wine and mint into a bowl and baste the turkey with the marinade every 20 minutes.

Cook for 3 hours. During the last 30 minutes place the mini sausages wrapped in the bacon around the turkey.

Serve with a gravy made from the turkey and basting juices.

Garnish with the mini pork sausages wrapped in streaky bacon and orange and lemon slices.

SERVES 10

120

Yorkshire Christmas Pie (Author's Recipe)

I could not resist this eighteenth-century recipe which I have converted for the Heartbeat Christmas spread, for I am sure this will be the highlight of somebody's table. It's quite expensive by today's standards but worth every sixpence. The pie consists of boned poultry fitted inside one another, starting with a turkey stuffed with goose which is stuffed with a chicken which is stuffed with a pigeon which is stuffed with a quail which is stuffed with sausage meat and hard boiled eggs! All this is encased in a pastry crust.

175g / 6oz of the following cooked and roughly chopped meats: turkey, goose, chicken and York ham
50g / 2oz butter
1 large onion, finely chopped
175g / 6oz button mushrooms
salt
freshly milled black pepper
6 tbsp brandy
300ml / 10 fl oz turkey stock
1 tsp cornflour blended with a tablespoon of port
150ml / 5 fl oz double cream
350g / 12oz shortcrust pastry (see page xx)
175g / 6oz sausage meat
4 hard boiled eggs, shelled
1 egg for washing the pastry

Pre-heat the oven gas mark 5, 190°C / 375°F.

Melt the butter in a large saucepan. Add the onion and mushrooms and cook for 4 minutes. Season well, add the brandy and turkey stock, simmer for 10 minutes, add the cornflour and double cream and simmer for 2 minutes. Remove from the heat and allow to cool.

Roll out the pastry on a lightly floured surface and use two thirds of it to line a 1.5 litre (two and half pint) pie dish.

Place the sausage meat on the bottom, line with the hard boiled eggs then the meat mixture.

Roll out the remaining pastry and cover the pie, pressing gently to seal all round. Brush the pie with the beaten egg and decorate with the trimmings.

Bake in the centre of the oven for 45-50 minutes.

Serve with baby roast potatoes, parsnips and mint peas.

SERVES 8-10

Venison Roast

This recipe takes three days to make and is Nick Rowan's favourite Christmas treat. It is also spectacular to look at. Garnished with fresh fruit and rowan jelly, this dish is irresitible.

3kg / 6lb venison haunch
1 large onion, chopped
2 garlic cloves, crushed
1 bouquet garni
8 black peppercorns
600ml / 20 fl oz red wine
150ml / 5 fl oz olive oil
2 tbsp seasoned flour
juice and rind of 2 oranges
juice and rind of 1 lemon
150ml / 5 fl oz apple juice
6 tbsp rowan jelly
4 tbsp port blended with 1 tbsp cornflour
freshly chopped parsley
50g / 2oz different varieties of red berries, hulled and washed

Pre-heat the oven to gas mark 3, 170°C / 325°F.

Trim any excess fat from the haunch. Place the onion, garlic, bouquet garni, peppercorns, wine and olive oil in a very large dish. Add the venison and baste with the marinade. Cover the dish completely with foil and place in the fridge for 2 days.

Strain the marinade and put to one side.

Brush the venison in oil and double wrap it in cooking foil and roast in the centre of the oven for 3 hours. Remove the foil half an hour before the end of the cooking time, sift over the flour and baste with the juices and turn the heat up to gas mark 4, 180°C / 350°F for the last 30 minutes.

Place the marinade into a saucepan and reduce by half. Add the juice and fruit rind to the apple juice and reduce that by half in the same saucepan. Add the rowan jelly, port and cornflour. Allow the sauce to simmer and thicken for 8 minutes.

Place the haunch on a large serving dish, pour the sauce around it and garnish with parsley and red berries. Serve with rowan jelly (see page 131).

SERVES 8-10

Braised Pork Fillet with Red Cabbage

A traditional Yorkshire recipe which marries the rich flavours of roast pork with the sweetish succulence of the cabbage.

4 x 450g / 1lb pork fillets
3 tbsp sesame oil
25g / 1oz butter
12 shallots, peeled
2 cloves garlic
450g / 1lb red cabbage, very finely shredded
salt
freshly milled black pepper
150ml / 5 fl oz sweet cider
2 sprigs of fresh thyme

Pre-heat the oven gas mark 5, 190°C / 375°F.

Clean the pork fillets, removing any excess fat. Put the oil and butter into a large frying pan and seal the pork fillets, cooking quickly all over for 4 minutes. Remove the fillets and place them in a deep oven casserole.

Add the shallots and garlic to the frying pan and cook for 5 minutes. Place them with the pork.

Quickly fry the red cabbage in the same pan for 6 minutes, seasoning well with salt and freshly milled black pepper.

Add the cider and cook for a further 8 minutes. Arrange the cabbage and all the juices over the pork fillets to completely cover them. Place the 2 sprigs of thyme onto the cabbage, cover with tin foil and braise in the centre of the oven for 35 minutes.

Remove the foil and discard the thyme. Transfer the red cabbage with a slotted spoon onto a large serving dish.

Slice the pork fillets and lay them on the top of the cabbage, garnished with the shallots.

SERVES 8-10

York Ham Glazed with Apricot Compôte

The perfect combination.

2kg / 4 lb York ham
1 onion stuck with 6 cloves
1 bay leaf
8 peppercorns
300ml / 10 fl oz sweet white wine
50g / 2oz soft brown sugar
175ml / 6 fl oz pureed apricots and juice
2 tbsp clear honey, warmed
275g / 10oz apricots sliced

Pre-heat the oven to gas mark 6, 200°C / 400°F.

Soak the ham in sufficient cold water to cover for 4 hours then discard the water.

Put the ham into a large saucepan with the onion, bay leaf, peppercorns and the white wine. Add sufficient cold water to cover. Bring to the boil, cover the pan and simmer gently for 2 hours.

Place the brown sugar, apricot puree and juice with the warmed honey into a bowl and mix together.

Strain the ham and remove the skin and score the fat into a diamond pattern. Place the ham on a baking tray and completely smother with the apricot compôte mixture.

Bake in the centre of the oven for 1 hour, basting every 15 minutes.

Place the York ham onto a serving dish, garnish with sliced apricots and the juices from the roasting tin.

SERVES 8-10

Pan-Fried Fillet Steak with Oyster Mushrooms

During the festive season people can become a little tired of turkey leftovers, so here's a beef recipe to boost jaded palates.

6 x 225g / 8oz fillet steaks, trimmed of all fat
salt
freshly milled black pepper
25g / 1oz butter
2 tbsp olive oil
75ml / 3 fl oz port
75ml / 3 fl oz beef stock
3 tbsp English mustard
150ml / 5 fl oz double cream
175ml / 6oz oyster mushrooms
roasted chestnuts

Pre-heat the oven to gas mark 6, 200°C / 400°F.

Season the steaks with the salt and freshly milled black pepper.

Heat the butter and oil in a heavy-bottomed, large frying pan on a medium heat.

Place the steaks into the pan and fry for 2 minutes on either side.

Pour over the port and beef stock and cook for a further minute on either side. Add the mustard, coating the tops of the steaks. Cook again for a further 2 minutes on either side. Remove the steaks to a heat-proof serving dish and keep them warm in a hot oven.

Add the cream to the juices left in the pan, blending them thoroughly. Add the sliced oyster mushrooms and cook for 3 minutes, tasting to adjust the seasoning.

Place the mushrooms around the steaks with the sauce and serve with a few roasted chestnuts.

SERVES 6

Rich Plum Pudding

I don't think Christmas is Christmas without plum pudding; and if this recipe is good enough for Nick Rowan then it's good enough for me.

25g / 1oz butter
100g / 4oz cooking apple, diced
200g / 7oz dried figs, chopped
100g / 4oz currants
100g / 4oz sultanas
225g / 8oz raisins
200g / 7oz blanched almonds, chopped
25g / 1oz hazelnuts, chopped
100g / 4oz Brazil nuts, chopped
175g / 6oz stale white breadcrumbs
1 tsp mixed spice
100g / 4oz soft brown sugar
100g / 4oz cut mixed peel
juice and rind of 1 lemon
100g / 4oz butter, softened
100g / 4oz clear honey, warmed
3 eggs beaten with 2 tbsp dark rum
3 tbsp brandy

Grease 2 large pudding basins.

Prepare a double steamer or 2 large saucepans to hold the pudding basins, three quarters full with water.

Put all the fruit with the dried fruits, nuts, breadcrumbs, spice, sugar, peel, lemon juice and rind into a large mixing bowl.

Melt the butter and honey in a saucepan on a very low heat. Allow to cool slightly and gently beat in the eggs and rum.

Pour the liquid over the dried ingredients, stirring thoroughly. Give a final stir and add the brandy.

Spoon the mixture into the greased basins, cover with greased paper and secure with string.

Place the basins into the steamers or pans, slowly bring the water to the boil. Cover and lower the heat, simmering for 3 hours. Top up with hot water when required.

Allow the plum pudding to settle for at least 4 hours, then steam again for a further hour before serving. Serve and garnish with a sprig of holly.

Put 3 tablespoons of brandy in a metal soup ladle and heat over a low flame. Ignite and pour over the pudding when serving, garnished with a sprig of holly.

SERVES 8 -10

Apple Pie with Wensleydale Cheese

Yorkshire folk like to see apple in their apple pie, not just a little sliver that's covered with pastry. When eating the apple pie it should be just warm, not hot, and – as it's Christmas – served with generous chunks of Wensleydale cheese and a glass of vintage port.

900g / 2 lb cooking apples, peeled, cored and thickly sliced
150g / 5oz soft brown sugar
1 tsp freshly grated nutmeg
1 tsp crushed cloves
milk to brush the pastry
1 tbsp caster sugar
450g / 1lb Wensleydale cheese
100g / 4oz white and black seedless grapes
50g / 2oz celery, cleaned and trimmed
50g / 2oz radish, trimmed

Shortcrust Pastry

350g / 12oz plain flour
pinch of salt
75ml / 3oz butter
75ml / 3oz lard

To make the pastry, sift the flour and salt into a large bowl, rub in the fat until it resembles fine breadcrumbs. Add just enough cold water to make a stiff dough (about 4-6 tablespoons).

Knead the pastry for 3 minutes then roll it out on a lightly floured surface, using two thirds to line a 900ml / one and half pint pie dish.

Pre-heat the oven gas mark 6, 200°C / 400°F.

Put half the apples into the dish, sprinkle with half the sugar, nutmeg and cloves, then top with the rest of the apples, nutmeg and cloves and sugar.

Cover with the remaining pastry, sealing the edges. Brush the pastry with a little milk and dredge with the caster sugar.

Bake in the centre of the oven for 20 minutes, then lower the heat to gas mark 4, 180°C / 350°F and bake for a further 15 minutes.

Serve warm with slices of Wensleydale cheese, grapes, celery and radish.

SERVES 8

Christmas Bread and Butter Pudding

Every Christmas the story's the same: there's always loads of leftover bread, bottles of milk and jars of mincemeat. So what better to do with all these than to turn them into a festive bread and butter pudding!

25g / 1oz butter
12 slices of buttered bread
50g / 2oz sultanas
400g / 14oz mincemeat, warmed
1 tsp freshly ground nutmeg
600ml / 20 fl oz milk
3 eggs
50g / 2oz soft brown sugar
brown sugar

Pre-heat the oven gas mark 4, 180°C / 350°F.

Grease a large baking dish with 25g / 1oz butter. Cut the bread into triangles and arrange in layers, buttered side up and sprinkled with sultanas. Spread mincemeat and grated nutmeg over the bread slices and finish with a top layer of bread.

Heat the milk in a saucepan but do not let it boil. Beat the eggs in a bowl with the sugar and whisk in the hot milk. Strain the custard mixture over the bread, finish with a little more grated nutmeg and a little more brown sugar.

Leave the dish to stand for 45 minutes. Bake in the centre of the oven for 35-40 minutes until the custard is set.

SERVES 8

Yorkshire Trifle

No jelly in this trifle and I promise you the flavour is far superior to the ready-made so-called trifles that are available in the shops today.

4 tbsp strawberry jam
275g / 10oz stale sponge cake
6 almond macaroons, crushed
150ml / 5 fl oz cream sherry
350ml / 12 fl oz milk
3 eggs
2 tbsp caster sugar
vanilla essence
150ml / 5 fl oz double cream, whipped

Spread the jam over the sponge cake and cut into small cubes. Arrange them in a large glass bowl. Add the crushed macaroons and pour over the sherry.

Put the milk into a saucepan and bring gently to the boil.

Into a bowl put the eggs and sugar, mixing them well. Slowly add the milk and a few drops vanilla essence, whisking briskly.

Strain the mixture into a clean saucepan and bring gently to boiling point. Simmer for 10 minutes on a very low heat until the custard thickens. Slowly pour the custard over the trifle base.

Leave the trifle for about 25 minutes until it cools. To prevent a skin forming, wet a piece of greaseproof paper and place it on the top of the custard.

When cold top with the whipped cream and serve.

SERVES 8

Nick Rowan's Merry Christmas Cake

The only way to get a kiss under the mistletoe from Nick Rowan is to praise his very rich Christmas cake. For a policeman he's really not a bad baker! Make this cake at least two weeks before Christmas.

225g / 8oz butter
225g / 8oz caster sugar
225g / 8oz plain flour, sifted with ½ tsp baking powder
pinch of salt
1 tsp mixed spice
6 eggs, whisked
450g / 1lb currants
225g / 8oz raisins
100g / 4oz glacé cherries, chopped
50g / 2oz chopped peel
100g / 4oz almonds, blanched, chopped
4 tbsp rum

Pre-heat the oven to gas mark 3, 170°C / 325°F.

Line a 10 inch cake tin with greaseproof paper.

Place the butter and sugar into a very large bowl and stir until completely blended.

Sift the flour with the baking powder, salt and mixed spice. Add the flour and then the egg mixture alternately, until both ingredients are used up.

Add the rest of the ingredients and stir until everything is completely blended.

Let the mixture settle for 1 hour, then give it a final stirring.

Put the mixture into the cake tin and cover the top with a piece of greaseproof paper.

Bake in the centre of the oven for 45 minutes. Lower the heat to gas mark 1, 140°C / 275°F for 4 hours.

Remove the cake and allow to cool completely before removing it from the tin.

Remove the paper. Turn the cake over and sprinkle the bottom with 4 tablespoons of brandy. Double wrap the cake in greasproof paper, then in cooking foil. Place the cake into a large biscuit tin and store in a cool place for at least a week before decorating and icing for Christmas.

SERVES 10-12

Chapter 11

Yorkshire Jams, Pickles and Preserves

What are the first things that spring to mind when jams, pickles and preserves are mentioned? Mouthwatering strawberry jam with juicy, fat fruit, tangy rowan jelly and sharp yet delicious piccalilli. When making jams and pickles, always choose fruit that is firm yet not overripe – if you pick fruit which is beyond its best then the jams will not set. When making gooseberry jam, use underripe gooseberries. When potting the preserves always make sure that the jars are clean, dry and warm. Fill the jars to the brim with preserves that are piping hot. Immediately cover the jars with greaseproof paper and seal with plastic coated twist tops while the preserves are still warm. Label and date each jar and store in a cool dry place. Most preserves will keep for up to twelve months if stored like this.

KATE'S HOME-MADE
STRAWBERRY JAM

YORKSHIRE RELISH

GOOSEBERRY AND
ELDERFLOWER JAM

PC ROWAN'S JELLY

LEMON CURD

PICCALILLI

PICKLED ONIONS

RED CABBAGE

PICKLED EGGS

VERUVIA'S RHUBARB
CHUTNEY

RASPBERRY VINEGAR AND
OTHER VINEGARS

Kate's Homemade Strawberry Jam

Fruits do vary in pectin and acid content, but you can now buy sugar with added pectin which ensures a perfectly set jam every time. If you are not over-fond of strawberries, replace them with the same amount of your favourite fruit.

1.4kg / 3lb strawberries
1.4kg / 3lb sugar with pectin
juice and rind of ½ lemon

Hull and wash the strawberries. Drain them well and cut them into quarters. Place the strawberries in a large bowl in layers with the sugar and pectin, leaving them for 3 hours. Put them into a large saucepan, add the lemon juice and rind and stir for 2 minutes until the lemon is blended. Boil rapidly for 5 minutes, then simmer for 15 minutes. Allow the jam to then cool for 15 minutes, removing any scum which forms on the surface. Stir the strawberries carefully through the jam. Pot into warm jars, cover, label and date. This jam will keep for 6 months.

MAKES 1.4 KG

Yorkshire Relish

This relish has been the favourite of Yorkshiremen for centuries. Naturally suspicious of meat covered in gravy, believing that they were being served with tarted up leftovers, Yorkshiremen would ask their local landlord for cold beef with Yorkshire relish on the side.

600ml / 20 fl oz malt vinegar
100g / 4oz soft brown sugar
1 tsp of salt
6 black peppercorns
25g / 1oz chillies, chopped
1 tbsp black treacle
1 tbsp Worcestershire sauce
1 tbsp mushroon ketchup
½ tsp freshly grated nutmeg

Place all the ingredients into a saucepan and bring to the boil. Simmer for 10 minutes then allow the relish to cool.

Pour into warm clean bottles with cork or vinegar proof tops.

This relish will keep for about 18 months if stored in a dry, dark place.

Goosesberry and Elderberry Jam

The gooseberries should be slightly underripe and all fruits washed thoroughly. You can use practically any summer fruits which take your fancy for this recipe.

900g / 2lb gooseberries
900g / 2lb elderberries
water to cover
2 tbsp lemon juice
2kg / 4½lb sugar with pectin

Wash the gooseberries and elderberries, topping and tailing them. Place in a large saucepan and add enough water to cover the fruit.

Bring the fruit to the boil and simmer for 30 minutes until the fruit is soft. Skim the top of the pan, add the lemon juice and sugar with pectin. Stir until the sugar is completely dissolved.

Rapidly bring to the boil until setting point is reached. This takes about 15 to 18 minutes.

Pot and seal the jam as before.

MAKES ABOUT 8LB JAM

PC Rowan's Jelly

I don't think rowan jelly was named after PC Nick, but I could be wrong! The rowan berries must be ripe and the apples sweet and juicy.

900g / 2lb rowan berries
900g / 2lb Cox's orange pippin
water to cover
2kg / 4½lb sugar with pectin

Remove any stalks from the rowan berries, wash and drain.

Peel, core and chop the apples.

Place the fruit into a large saucepan and cover the fruit with water. Cook for 15 minutes, then strain the fruit and liquid through a fine sieve into another clean saucepan. Add the sugar and pectin. Boil rapidly for 15 minutes until the jelly is at setting point. Pot and seal in warm jars.

This is excellent with any of the Game recipes in this book.

Lemon Curd

This is always served at lunch and tea, and not just on buttered bread but on cakes and scones as well.

juice and rind of 4 large lemons
225g / 8oz butter, softened
450g / 1lb caster sugar
5 large eggs, beaten

Place the lemon juice and grated rind into a bowl over a saucepan of boiling water.

Whisk in the softened butter and sugar over a low heat until the mixture has completely dissolved.

Take the pan from the heat and allow it to cool for 30 seconds. Whisk in the beaten eggs. Return the pan to the heat and cook gently again for 5 to 8 minutes until the curd coats the back of the spoon.

Pot and seal the curd.

MAKES 900G / 2LB

Piccalilli

If you had walked into any Yorkshire home in the 1960s I guarantee that you would have seen a jar of piccalilli on every table. Back then, it was a good way of using up end-of-season vegetables, but nowadays, of course, you can buy the same vegetables from the supermarket all year round.

900g / 2lb equal mixture of the following vegetables cut into bite size pieces: gherkins, baby onions (peeled) and cauliflower florets.
75g / 3oz cooking salt
600ml / 20 fl oz white vinegar
175g / 6oz granulated sugar
50g / 2oz dried English mustard powder
1 tsp turmeric
25g / 1oz cornflour

Put the vegetables into a large dish and sprinkle with the salt, cover and leave it to stand for 24 hours.

Wash and rinse the vegetables. Put the vinegar in a separate large saucepan and heat gently. Add the vegetables.

Mix together all the dry ingredients and add to the vegetables and vinegar. Simmer gently for 15 minutes.

Pot and seal with vinegar proof tops. Leave for at least 2 months before using.

Pickled Onions

I like my pickled onions to taste quite sweet so I use a milder vinegar than the pickling vinegar you buy in the supermarkets. White wine vinegar isn't quite as sharp and if you add in a couple of tablespoons of soft brown sugar, then the tanginess of the vinegar is mellowed even more. To make a spiced vinegar add 8 cloves, 12g / ½oz pieces of ginger, a couple of cinnamon sticks and 8 white peppercorns to 1 litre of malt vinegar. Bottle for 2 months but shake the bottle every week. Strain and use when required.

900g / 2 lb pickling onions, peeled
600ml / 20 fl oz spiced or pickling vinegar, hot but not boiling
100g / 4oz soft brown sugar.
12g / ½oz salt
1 tsp pink peppercorns

Put all the ingredients into a bowl stir with a wooden spoon until the sugar dissolves. Pack the pickles into jars and top up with the vinegar. Seal with vinegar proof tops and leave them to stand for at least 4 to 6 weeks before using them.

Red Cabbage

Served with Aidensfield tattie pie (recipe on page 85), this home-made red cabbage will become the talking point of the table. Choose a really firm cabbage and remove all the discoloured leaves. Cut the cabbage into quarters and cut out the inner stalk. You are now ready to begin.

1 red cabbage, washed and shredded
100g / 4oz cooking salt
50g / 2oz soft brown sugar
600ml / 20 fl oz white wine vinegar

Place the shredded cabbage, salt and sugar into layers in a large basin. Cover with clingfilm and leave to stand for 24 hours.

Rinse the cabbage in cold water, draining it well. Pack the cabbage into jars, cover with the white wine vinegar and seal.

Let the red cabbage stand for at least 7 days before using but use it within 3 months or it will lose its crispness.

133

Pickled Eggs

I once saw a Chinese pickled egg sold off at an auction for £1,000. The buyer then proceeded to eat it there and then. My pickled eggs cost considerably less to make. They should be boiled for 10 minutes. A tip is to stir them after three minutes. This centralizes the yolks. Once the eggs have boiled, plunge them into cold water for two minutes before shelling them.

12 eggs, hard boiled and shelled
600ml / 20 fl oz white wine vinegar
3 blades of mace

Pack the eggs into glass jars, cover with the vinegar and add a blade of mace to each jar.

Seal and leave for 1 month before using.

Veruvia's Rhubarb Chutney

Heartbeat would not be the same without a jar of rhubarb chutney constantly on Veruvia's table.

450g / 1lb rhubarb (red end), washed and chopped
2 onions, chopped
3 tbsp sultanas
2 tbsp soft brown sugar
pinch of cayenne pepper
1 tsp salt
1 tbsp mild curry paste
2 tbsp port
150ml / 5 fl oz white wine vinegar

Put all the ingredients into a large saucepan, bring to the boil and simmer slowly for 10 minutes, stirring all the time. Boil rapidly for a further 5 minutes until the rhubarb is fully cooked.

Put into warm jars and let it stand for 7 days before using.

This chutney is made for the Lamb burgers (see page 44) in this book.

Raspberry Vinegar

This is the vinegar Yorkshiremen will die for. They often shake a few drops over their Yorkshire pudding and their chips, and once you've tried it I'm sure you will end up doing the same!

900g / 2lb fresh raspberries
2 litres white wine vinegar
900g / 2lb granulated sugar

Put the hulled raspberries into a large clean glass bowl. Pour over enough vinegar to cover the raspberries. Cover and leave them to stand for 4 days, stirring every day.

Strain the liquid but not the raspberries through a non-metalic sieve. Pour the juice into a saucepan, add the sugar, bring the juice to the boil and then simmer for 20 minutes. Let the liquid stand until it is completely cold and then bottle, using cork or plastic tops. Seal and let it stand for at least 4 days before use.

You can use this same method and recipe with any soft fruit.

Chapter 12

Gravy and Sauces

The point of any sauce is to enhance the flavours of a dish rather than to smother them. Gravies and sauces have a glorious history in English cooking and I have selected eight delicious traditional recipes to conclude our feast of Heartbeat country cooking!

PERFECT GRAVY

OLD ENGLISH GAME SAUCE

APPLE SAUCE

BREAD SAUCE

GOOSBERRY SAUCE

TRADITIONAL CUSTARD
SAUCE

OLD-FASHIONED ENGLISH
BUTTERSCOTCH SAUCE

RUM OR BRANDY SAUCE

Perfect Gravy

When I want to serve onion gravy with Yorkshire puddings, I just add the juice from the roast beef to this recipe with an extra finely chopped onion. This recipe is dedicated to Francis Coulson.

50g / 2oz beef dripping
1 onion, finely diced
1 carrot, finely diced
2 rashers best back bacon,
rind and any gristle removed and finely chopped
2 tbsp dry sherry
2 tbsp red wine vinegar
50g / 2oz plain flour
600ml / 1 pint meat stock
1 bouquet garni
1 tbsp tomato purrée
salt and freshly milled black pepper

Melt the dripping in a heavy based saucepan over a medium heat. Add the onion, carrot and bacon and fry for 10 minutes until light brown, stirring frequently. Add the sherry and vinegar and continue cooking for 3 minutes.

Blend in the flour, stirring the roux for 10-12 minutes until it is brown. Gradually add half the beef stock, stirring constantly until the mixture has cooked through and thickened. Bring to the boil and add the bouquet garni, then lower the heat and simmer, uncovered, for 30 minutes. Stir in the tomato puree, remaining beef stock and salt and pepper, then continue simmering and skimming the surface as necessary for a further 30 minutes. Taste and adjust the seasoning all the time.

Strain through a fine non-metallic sieve, skim off any extra fat and serve.

MAKES ABOUT 600ML / 1 PINT

Variation: Light Tomato Sauce
Just add an extra 100g / 4oz tomato puree to the perfect gravy recipe to make a light tomato sauce. Serve with chicken, veal and steaks.

Old English Game Sauce

For this modern game sauce, I have borrowed from the genius of Charles Elme Francatelli's venison sauce, which he made for Queen Victoria when he was her personal chef. Makes about 225ml / 8 fl oz.

2 tbsp orange and green peppercorn vinegar
200g / 7oz redcurrant jelly
2 tbsp port
1 blade of mace
1 small stick of cinnamon
1 bay leaf
1 tbsp chopped lemon rind
25g / 1oz mushrooms, coarsely chopped
1 tbsp capers, finely chopped
pinch of salt
2 shallots, finely chopped
4 black and 4 white peppercorns, freshly milled

Put the orange and green pepper vinegar, redcurrant jelly, Port, mace, cinnamon, bay leaf, lemon rind and finely chopped shallots into a saucepan over a high heat and bring to the boil. Reduce the heat and simmer for 12 minutes, then add the salt.

Pass the sauce through a fine non-metallic sieve into a sauce boat. Sprinkle with the mushrooms, capers and freshly milled peppercorns, blending them into the sauce before serving.

MAKES ABOUT 225ML / 8 FLOZ

Apple Sauce

The great British pork sauce recipe.

15g / ½oz butter
450g/ 1lb Bramley apples, peeled, cored and chopped
2 tbsp water
2 tbsp caster sugar
1 tsp tarragon vinegar
pinch of ground cloves
salt and freshly ground black pepper

Melt the butter in a saucepan over a medium heat, then add the apples with the water. Cover and cook gently for 8 minutes.

Remove the pan from the heat and mash the apples to a soft smooth mixture. Stir in the sugar, vinegar and cloves. Re-heat, stirring all the time. Taste and adjust the seasoning.

MAKES ABOUT 400G / 14OZ.

Bread Sauce

This sauce came into being in medieval times when bread was a staple food so breadcrumbs were plentiful, and flour wasn't yet used as a thickener. It has never gone out of fashion, and is still a regular feature of Christmas feasts. In Elizabeth Raffald's The Experienced English Housekeeper *this recipe for bread sauce is listed as Sauce for a Turkey:*

"*Cut the crust off a penny-loaf, cut the rest in thin slices, put in cold water, with a few peppercorns, a little salt and onion, boil it till the bread is quite soft, then heat it well, put in a quarter of a pound of butter, two spoonfuls of thick cream, and put into a basin.* **"**

I think my 20th-century version of bread sauce is excellent with game, roast chicken and, of course, the traditional roast turkey for Christmas dinner. Bread sauce should never be re-boiled and take care not to over-cook it or it will become a 'gooey' mess.

6 cloves
1 onion, peeled
450ml /15 fl oz milk
pinch of mace
4 black peppercorns
225g /8oz fresh white breadcrumbs
15g / ½oz butter
2 tbsp double cream
salt and freshly milled black pepper

Stick the cloves into the onion, then put the onion into a saucepan with the milk, mace and peppercorns. Bring to the boil, then remove the pan from the heat, cover and leave the milk to infuse for 35 minutes.

Strain the milk through a fine sieve into another clean pan and stir in the breadcrumbs. Return the pan to the heat and stir continuously for 4-6 minutes until the mixture becomes quite thick.

Season the sauce well, then stir in the cream and butter. Taste and adjust the seasoning if necessary. Serve warm.

MAKES ABOUT 400G / 14OZ.

MAKES ABOUT 400G / 14OZ.
Gooseberry Sauce

This classic sauce dates back to the seventeenth century, and has always been served with mackerel. For a stronger-flavoured sauce, use fish stock instead of water when stewing the gooseberries.

225g / 8oz gooseberries
150ml / 5 fl oz water
25g / 1oz butter
25g / 1oz sugar
juice of 1 lemon
freshly grated nutmeg
fresh snipped chives and finely chopped fresh sorrel (optional)
salt and freshly milled black pepper

Slowly stew gooseberries very gently with the water and butter until they are pulpy, then beat them with a wire whisk until a smooth sauce forms.

Re-heat the sauce and stir in the sugar, lemon juice and nutmeg to taste. Taste and adjust the seasoning. Add a few chives or some sorrel if you desire.

MAKES ABOUT 200G/7OZ.

Traditional Custard Sauce

Let's not forget the easy things in life! If the custard does become too hot and curdles, remove it from the heat and immediately whisk in another egg yolk.

2 egg yolks, size 3, lightly beaten
25g / 1oz caster sugar
3 drops of vanilla essence
300ml / 10 fl oz boiling milk
150ml / 5 fl oz double cream (optional)

Mix the egg yolks, sugar and vanilla essence in a large clean bowl. Whisk in the boiling milk, then return the custard to the saucepan over a low heat, stirring all the time with a wooden spoon until the custard becomes thick enough to coat the back of the spoon. Do not let the mixture boil or the eggs will scramble.

If you want extra creaminess, stir in the cream just before you take the custard off the heat. Serve at once, or leave to cool completely, cover and refrigerate for up to 2 days to serve chilled.

MAKES ABOUT 300ML / 10FL OZ

Variations
Christmas Brandy Custard Sauce: Use the ingredients and method above, but omit the vanilla essence and stir in 3 tablespoons brandy.
Whisky or Rum Custard Sauce: Omit the vanilla and stir in 2 tablespoons whisky or rum at the end of the simmering time and whisk gently together.

Old-Fashioned English Butterscotch Sauce

225g/8oz light brown sugar
1 tbsp golden syrup
50g / 2oz butter
3 tbsp double cream
1 tsp vanilla essence

Put the sugar and golden syrup in a saucepan over a medium heat and stir to dissolve the sugar. Add the butter and bring to the boil, then lower the heat and simmer for 10 minutes until the sauce is really thick. Remove the pan from the heat and stir in the cream and vanilla essence.

MAKES ABOUT 300ML / 10 FL OZ.

Rum or Brandy Sauce

Here's one of my favourite sauces for Christmas. I find Christmas sauces always bring out the worst in the cook, but the best in the people tasting the sauce. It really does no good for the cook to be tempted to say 'it's Christmas, so I'll double the amount of spirit' because it will only ruin the sauce. (Michael Smith, the former English cookery writer, used to make a delicious version of this using 3 tablespoons of Jamaican dark rum.) Makes about 600ml/1 pint.

50g / 2oz butter
25g/ 1oz plain flour
600ml / 1 pint milk, warm
2 tbsp caster sugar
3 tbsp rum or brandy

Melt the butter in a saucepan over a medium heat, then sprinkle in the flour and use a wooden spoon to stir together to form a roux. Slowly stir in the warm milk, stirring all the time.

Sprinkle with the sugar and continue simmering for 8 minutes, stirring all the time. Add the rum or brandy and continue simmering for a further 5 minutes, stirring all the time to prevent the sauce sticking.

Index